PRAISE FOR ERIN POWER

"Girl Power will last a lifetime with any girl who goes through the program. It will last with the parents as well, because what goes on are great opportunities for discussions between a parent and a girl."

—SHERENE, MASTER'S DEGREE IN EDUCATIONAL PSYCHOLOGY

"Thanks once again for a wonderful evening with our girls. They simply love you. We talked about what they learned and they talked on and on. You are doing really important work: motivator, role model, friend, teacher. We are blessed to have you in our girls' lives."

—ANNE C., RN BC MSN ANP, NURSE EDUCATOR

"Thanks Auntie for loving me enough to start this great program!"

—GABY, GIRL POWER GIRL

"I really liked the class and want to go again. It made me feel strong, proud, awesome and undefeated! Thank you Miss Erin, you're the best teacher EVER!!!"

—ALINA, GIRL POWER GIRL

"My daughter had a fantastic experience. Girl Power is all about promoting healthy minds and bodies in girls by learning great exercises, healthy eating habits, empowerment messages, etc. Erin is full of positive energy, enthusiasm and fun, which is contagious! The girls leave every class rejuvenated and excited. My daughter still talks about her wonderful experience in Girl Power!"

—ASHLEY, GIRL POWER MOM

"Girl Power helped my daughter appreciate the 'girl' inside. She now realizes that she is not a tomboy but an AMAZING girl athlete! Thank you Erin for giving so much of yourself to help our strong, smart and AMAZING girls!"

—MICHELLE, GIRL POWER MOM

"Thank you Erin for offering such a valuable class to our girls!"

—TALEEN, GIRL POWER MOM

"Thank you for being part of our troop's success!"

—LEE BURNS, LEADER TO HOPKINTON GIRL SCOUT
TROOP 72975

"The Girl Power Program is a wonderful inspirational program for girls, teenagers and young women. I have been a Girl Power Instructor for three years and I am honored to be part of it! This program focuses on teaching with a loving heart many life fundamentals such as how to be a good friend, how to be independent and how to make healthy choices. A few of the foundational principles being taught include honesty, trustworthiness, and respect for oneself and others. There are many different activities in the program that are designed to build self-esteem and confidence including arts and crafts, physical fitness, games, and motivational encouragement. The program also helps the students develop useful tools like healthy eating charts and sleep preparation guidelines.

"I have seen first-hand how this program can motivate and transform the girls into fearless warriors. Often new participants come into the program feeling shy, quiet, and unsure, but gradually the principles covered in the program help empower the students to build new relationships and transform them into confident and powerful girls. Witnessing the students learn and grow is very exciting to see and I am always grateful to help facilitate this change as a Girl Power Instructor!"

—ANN M, GIRL POWER, YOGA, SPINNING INSTRUCTOR
AND HEALING PRACTITIONER

"Girl Power brings such a positive energy and focus on loving yourself from the inside out. It reinforces to young girls to be confident, strong, and that true beauty comes from a kind soul. It's an empowering, beautiful experience that I'm happy my daughter had the opportunity to participate in!"

—CAITLIN THEODOROU, GIRL POWER MOM

"I was introduced to Erin Mahoney's Girl Power program three years ago when she spoke for the first time to my daughter's Girl Scout troop. The powerful, enthusiastic, and positive messages she has given these girls will guide them as they continue to grow into strong confident young ladies. It has been a pleasure working with Erin as she tailors these messages to fit the needs each year for my group. Erin lives her life as an example for all girls."

—MEGHAN KIRBY, GIRL SCOUT LEADER AND GIRL POWER MOM

"It's fun. I love her activities. The Name Game and the Healthy Eating Food Challenge are my favorites!"

—LEAH, AGE 9, GIRL POWER GIRL

"Hats off to Erin Mahoney for creating a positively enriching and empowering program for young girls! When my daughter was in 1st grade she participated in Girl Power. Now in 3rd grade she still talks about her experience! Some of her favorite memories were the Brave and Courageous class when she painted warrior paint on her face. Not only was it a fun and silly class but she also took home the valuable life lesson that she has the power to be the best that she can be, always! She also loved doing yoga and learning new poses. Her favorite part was at the end when Erin gave her an envelope with colorful printed-out characteristics specifically picked for her. My daughter still has those characteristics hanging on her wall to read every day. As a mother of a young girl I can't think of a better way for my daughter to spend her time after school. Erin Mahoney is a true blessing with an energy so positive you can feel it seep into your soul."

—YVONNE FROHN, GIRL POWER MOM

"I was lucky enough to be introduced to Girl Power two years ago. After attending one of the Girl Power classes, I knew this was something I needed to be involved in! The energy of every lesson Erin created is well thought-out and extremely effective. The activities and messages are well received by the girls all while having an amazing time! I believe with all that is expected from our girls today, Girl Power reinforces how important it is for them to believe in themselves!"

—MOREEN HARDCASTLE, GIRL POWER MOM AND GIRL POWER INSTRUCTOR

"After Part 1, the girls were so enthusiastic about Girl Power that they couldn't wait for Part 2. They happily talked amongst themselves about the program and then shared their well thought out feedback with Kristine and I. It was impressive how well they internalized the ideas that Erin was trying to impress upon them. I think they grasped and retained the information because of the way it was presented to them. Erin made learning fun! The affirmations the girls exclaimed gave me goose bumps: "I am strong! I am smart! I am pretty! I am amazing!" The girls earned a "My Best Self" badge and a "Girl Power" fun badge. They also gained a beneficial dose of self-esteem and empowerment. Bottom line—I loved this program and will be calling on Erin again in the future. I highly recommend Girl Power. I can't say enough about it."

—MARIA B.

GIRL SCOUT BROWNIE TROOP 30851 CO-LEADER AND MOM OF TWO VERY STRONG, SMART, PRETTY, AMAZING GIRLS

girl power

BOOKS BY ERIN C. MAHONEY

*GIRL POWER GUIDEBOOK FOR PARENTS AND INSTRUCTORS:
THE PROGRAM, STRATEGIES AND INSIGHTS THAT
TRANSFORM AND EMPOWER GIRLS*

GIRL POWER JOURNAL: BE STRONG. BE SMART. BE AMAZING!

Guidebook for Parents and Instructors

The Program, Strategies, and Insights that Transform and Empower Girls

Recommended Ages 8 through 13

ERIN C. MAHONEY

with RODNEY MILES

Girl Power Go

Copyright © 2017 by Erin C. Mahoney
All rights reserved

Published by Girl Power Go, LLC

No part of this book may be reproduced in any manner
without written permission except in the case of brief
quotations embodied in critical articles and reviews.

For information about special discounts for bulk purchases
or author interviews, appearances, and speaking engagements
please contact the author via: www.girlpowergo.com and
info@girlpowergo.com

First Edition

Collaboration, consulting, editing, cover and book design by
Rodney Miles: www.RodneyMiles.com
Illustrations (including cover and interior illustrations of the
Girl Power Journal) by Keith Seidel: www.KeithSeidel.com
Girl Power logo designed by Keith Weilding
All photographs by the author unless noted otherwise.

The information in this book is meant to supplement, not replace, proper training. As with any sport involving speed, equipment, balance and environmental factors, there may be some inherent risk. The authors and publisher advise readers to take full responsibility for their safety and that of the girls instructed, and to also know their limits. Before practicing the skills described in this book, be sure that your equipment is well maintained, and do not take risks beyond your girls' level of experience, aptitude, training, and comfort level.

The first Girl Power class ever delivered, in my girlfriend's basement, to my niece's Girl Scout troop.

Dedication

ℬ

This book is dedicated to my mother Danielle.

You were the strongest woman I ever knew.

Your strength, passion, and love live on inside of me. They are in everything I do! This book shares so many of the life lessons you taught me.

I miss you every day of my life but your spirit continues to inspire and bring love and care to others.

It's also dedicated to every girl and every woman who ever doubted themselves, ever felt afraid or alone; to every girl and woman that lacks self confidence, self-love, and the solid belief that they are powerful and strong even in their weakest moments.

I have been where you are and this book is for you! You have everything you need within you already to be absolutely amazing!

GET MORE GIRL POWER!

Bring Girl Power programs to your community or area!

Get cool Girl Power gear!

See ongoing live and online Girl Power programs
for young girls and women!

Become a Girl Power Go Certified Instructor!

Attend a Girl Power conference or retreat,
Meet Erin, and learn empowerment strategies
directly from her and her team!

Go to www.GirlPowerGo.com/Extras and get updated
information and news, see videos of actual Girl Power
classes, and get even more positive Girl Power vibes!

Acknowledgements

৯১

TO MY AMAZING HUSBAND Brian. Words cannot possibly express the love and gratitude I feel to have you in my corner. Your patience and support rock my world! You are a gift in every way. The life we share makes me feel as if anything is possible! Thank you for always knowing that this book *would* get finished, even when I was unsure.

Jack and Joey, you are the two most wonderful things I have ever created. You have watched me work hard and have given me time and space to create when it wasn't always easy. You have taught me so many things about how to love and care for another human being. You give me countless opportunities to learn, grow, and change. There is no greater gift than being your mother. I am proud of you and know you are proud of me!

Jon Daskam, your positive outlook and genuine belief in me made me continue. Your deep connection and belief in this work that I do *are the reasons* that I did not quit. You always reminded me of how important this work of empowering young girls and women is. I am full of gratitude for you and our "working/brainstorming/support" sessions.

Michelle, my only sister, biggest cheerleader, loving friend, you are a blessing and you gave us our special "Gaby" girl! You are my best friend and Mom would be so proud of us! Thank you for believing in me always and for telling me to "put it on paper and we will make it happen!" If not for you and those words Girl Power may have never entered schools in the after school programming arena. Because of you, your belief in me and this program, we have impacted thousands of girls and for that I am eternally grateful. "Thank you" doesn't even begin to cover it! I love you so much—xoxo!

Sean Roach, without our chance meeting at a conference in March of 2015 these books would not exist! I am forever grateful that I found myself in the audience when you spoke. You talked about books and how people need to find their niche and then use books to get their ideas out to the world. I had my niche for years but never thought about putting it into a book. I will NEVER forget pulling you aside and asking for a few minutes of your time to tell you about my "Girl Power" program. You graciously listened to me tell you all about this thing that I created and how I wanted to spread this mission and message of empowering girls through love, kindness, and fitness nationwide. I said, "I'm a big thinker you know." I shared that I didn't want to franchise but that I was looking for a vehicle to share these stories and lessons of empowerment. You then told me that I was *not* a big thinker. I was a bit taken back until you went on to say, "You need to write a book, translate it in every language and go global!" Holy crap, I thought, "This guy isn't messing around and he is a BIG thinker. I have to work with this man!" Well, the rest is history. I signed up for your Expert Catapult program that day and began this project of writing books. Thank you for holding nothing back and giving me the challenge to "think global" and really go for it!

Thank you to Margaret Lynch. It was at your Ignite conference in Boston in March 2015 that I met Sean Roach and began the journey of writing these books. You and the work that you do introduced me to Tapping and EFT (Emotional Freedom Technique) which has been instrumental in my shift to focus on Girl Power exclusively in my business. It was the shift of energy and deep desire to have positive impact on the world that lead me to where I am and the creation of these books. Keep doing what you are doing, it's amazing and was life changing for me!

Keith Seidel, your illustrations bring the characters in my books to life. Some of them are real, living people with personalities and others developed from our discussions and your incredible imagination. The lessons they are teaching others through these books existed for a very long time, if only in my head. You somehow took my vision of what the characters would bring to the Girl Power story and made it a reality. They are just as amazing and powerful as I had imagined they would be. At times we would discuss a class situation and how the girls would react to the lesson plan. Your illustrations made me feel like you were in the classroom with me, interacting with the students, and that completely blows my mind! You listened to my ideas and created *exactly* what I asked for and then some. Thank you for sharing your incredible talent with us in these books and for bringing the Girl Power Go characters that I love so deeply to life.

Rodney Miles, thank you for helping me to make these books a reality. I didn't know where to begin or how it would end. It's been a great ride and I know it's only the beginning! You my friend and editor are talented, kind, and a rock star in my book! Literally! Thank you for helping me to make it happen so that we can now share this book's lessons and "energy" with the world!

CONTENTS

FOREWORD

by CHRISTINE BASILE

NOISY, COMPETITIVE, I was born to a big, Irish-Italian family. Our household was all about discipline and teamwork. A lot of parental support, they kept an eye on what we were doing and expected us to do well, they had high expectations for us. I went through Catholic schools as a child—my mom thought it was important for us to have that discipline. And I was a mischievous kid, so I think that's why my mom felt so strongly about discipline. I have an older sister and four boys after me. My older sister was a mother's dream—did everything she was supposed to do, did it perfectly, did it on-time, did it right. Very smart. She ended up the salutatorian of her class.

Then came me. I was not interested in school except that I got to meet kids my own age. We lived in a big, busy neighborhood with plenty of kids. Lots of big families on our street—on Grove Street—and we played together every day, all day. We played every sport, everybody was included, and it was a very active childhood. It was a blast for me. The only thing that was tough was that I wanted to play everything *with* the boys. My mother did not approve. She wanted me to not be so athletic, so aggressive, so fun-loving. I was, in my mother's words, "bold." I was probably not what she wanted in the 1950s and 1960s in a little girl. I didn't care about "pink." I just wore anything that I could wear, whether it was jeans or a t-shirt, as long as I could play games. So my mother was my first challenge in life because I didn't fit the mold she had in mind for me, didn't fit the model.

And I just loved sports—*just loved them*. And I bring up school because decades ago the Catholic school had very different expectations for boys than for girls, and different ideas of what each should be exposed to. For instance, on the playground our play area was divided by a big line—boys on one side, girls on the other. If you were in third grade or above, there was a big crosswalk where you could go across to the big field, and across the field was the baseball field; a little pond (which was always exciting to me); a blacktop area for basketball courts; and girls weren't allowed over there, just the boys were. So it was there that I had my first "Rosa Parks" incident. I wore my shorts under my uniform one day, and at recess walked across with the boys, took my skirt off at the other side and hung it on a tree, had my shorts on underneath, went and played, and had the best recess of my life—didn't think twice about it, had a blast! Played the whole recess. The nuns came out and rang the bell. We lined up, I put my skirt back on, and the principal was waiting for me on the other side of the street.

I received the "golden ruler" on one hand and she gave me another few swipes across the knuckles on the other hand because I didn't cry the way she expected me to. But you know what? It was worth going across the street. And what I learned then, as a young child, is that we weren't all given the opportunity to do everything. So as a young person going all through school, I was always wanting to do things like Little League, I was always wanting to do things that were for "boys only."

So I grow older, life goes on, and I decide in high school that I'll become a very good student and a very good athlete, and I realize that what I want to do is create for young girls the opportunity that I never had. And as a result when I was in college as an undergraduate studying physical education and health, I went back to my hometown and I created softball teams for girls, I made sure they had tennis tournaments, that they had road races, and that everything that was open to boys was open to girls as well. That's what made me happy, that I would make sure that those girls had the opportunities that I never did, and had good coaching—people that enjoyed the sport, people that were trained in the sport. It was the experience as a young girl of being told, "No, you can't do this. You can't play Little League. You can't do this, you can't do that," that ultimately became my calling as a professional, which was to be a physical educator and a coach.

I personally had many different athletic achievements at the high school level, in basketball and softball—those were the only two sports available for girls at the time. I went to U-Mass, Amherst, and played varsity basketball as a freshman, and played varsity softball. I was actually bored by varsity softball my sophomore year because I had played so much ASA[1] softball in the summers, that I learned the game of lacrosse and played lacrosse at the varsity level my junior and senior years. When I graduated I chose a job down in Englewood, New Jersey. I taught health and physical education, and coached field hockey, basketball, and lacrosse. I stayed there three years and in my final year there, became a co-athletic director with another young colleague and helped raise the level of play and financial support for the girls' sports programs at the Dwight-Englewood School.

I then took a job at the University of New Hampshire in Durham as the assistant woman's athletic director, and assistant women's basketball coach—the first person to hold that position. I did that for three years. From my connections there and from the work I did as an administrator and coach, I was then asked to be the head women's basketball coach at Boston University. I did that job down at BU from 1983 through 1999. It was very challenging. We won some championships and I had some players go on and play professional ball in England, Australia, and different countries. But in 1999 it wasn't fun for me anymore. I didn't

---

[1] The "ASA" and "ASA/USA" is the Amateur Softball Association, the "National Governing Body of Softball" with over three million members —Wikipedia

accept the renewal of my contract. I went on a soul-searching trip and hiked the Grand Canyon, then decided I was going to go back to what I loved to do, which was teaching. And here I am in Hopkinton, Massachusetts, at the elementary level, at the Elmwood School, which is only second and third grade.

I first *heard* Erin Mahoney though the walls at Elmwood, in the gym talking with the girls, and I'm always curious about what's going on in our building. I had never seen a woman working with the girls, specifically. We had a lot of after-school activities—karate, basketball, flag football—but never a group that had *just girls*. So I was curious. I went up to Erin and asked, "Hey, what's going on here?" I would come to find out she was the aunt of one of the little girls (Gaby) I had in class a few years earlier. As time went on, Erin was at a health fair, where she had a Girl Power kiosk. We talked about Girl Power a little more and she talked to me about her background. I was curious as to how she arrived at what she was going to teach those young people. I was all for it because I had always wished I'd had a mentor and I never did.

As a young coach I would just go and watch different people coach in all different sports. I'd ask if I could come and observe; I'd interview them; and I'd read every article I could find to learn more about the profession. Nowadays there are more resources available for young girls to become empowered and these kinds of things, but back then you were more of a *survivor* than you were a young, talented girl. You just had to learn on your own, the *hard way*, at the "School of Hard Knocks" because you had to overcome a great deal in order to achieve your goals. Things weren't really set up in athletics for girls to be successful—not in my town, anyway. There's no way we are going to have peace and success on Earth if half the people are not allowed to do things that they think are healthy for them. And I think that's what was happening to us.

So I was excited about what Erin was doing. And today everything has changed, the world is different. So for these young people at our school—which is only second and third grade—for them to be talking about these things, and to believe in themselves and that they can do anything—holy smokes! I think that's just amazing. It's very different from my upbringing.

When I was a Division 1 women's basketball coach, probably 90 percent of all the head coaches were women. Now it's less than 50 percent. Before Title IX[2] came through—don't ask me why, I suppose it was just old economics—the women's programs did not get much support. When Title IX came through and they *had* to put more money in, they started pouring more money into salaries and recruiting, and the programs that received more money were very successful, as with the University of Tennessee and Old Dominion. There were certain programs across the country where the women's programs just took off—North Carolina, Chapel Hill, for example. The programs

---

[2] "Title IX states that: No person in the United States shall, on the basis of sex, be excluded from participation in, be denied the benefits of, or be subjected to discrimination under any education program or activity receiving Federal financial assistance." — www2.ed.gov/about/.../tix_dis.html

that were given those opportunities *blossomed,* and much faster than anybody expected. So once the engine started turning and people realized, "Wow, they *are* going to support women's sports," then, slowly, the support systems came into place. But as the earnings went up with the salaries, more men were interested. And men being the administrators, hired *other men,* and that's what happened.

At Boston University the men that were there, probably as much as the women that were there, helped me only because they knew my work from UNH. Rick Pitino[3] was just leaving—I think he was going to the Knicks—and he knew me from camps. He knew how hard I had worked. Rick went in and talked to the athletic director, who later told me, "When Rick came in he said, 'You have to hire this young person. She's a whippersnapper and this is the kind of person

---

[3] "Richard Andrew 'Rick' Pitino (born September 18, 1952) is an American basketball coach. Since 2001, he has been the head coach at the University of Louisville, and coached the Cardinals to the 2013 NCAA Men's Division I Basketball Championship. As a college head coach, Pitino has also served at Boston University, Providence College and the University of Kentucky, leading that program to the NCAA championship in 1996. In addition to his college coaching career, Pitino also served two stints in the NBA, coaching the New York Knicks for two seasons and the Boston Celtics for three and a partial fourth. Pitino holds the distinction of being the only recognized men's coach in NCAA history to lead three different schools (Providence, Kentucky, and Louisville) to a Final Four and the only coach in the NCAA to lead two different schools to an NCAA National Championship (Kentucky and Louisville). Pitino is also one of only four coaches in NCAA history . . . to take his school to the Final Four in four separate decades, one of only three coaches . . . to have led two different programs to at least two Final Fours each, and one of only two coaches . . . to have led two different programs to at least three Final Fours each." —Wikipedia

we need in this program.'" When I was interviewed everybody spoke very highly but it was interesting—it was still the male model of leadership.

When I received my first contract at Boston University it was because the football coach had become the athletic director and I remember him very clearly. He called me into his office and he said, "Chris, I don't see you as a woman coach, I see you as a coach who happens to be a woman." I was like—wow! In coaching, that was a really big compliment. Some people might be upset by that, but I understood what he was saying. He was telling me, "You're taking this as a calling and a profession, and you're working just as hard as anyone else. You're one of us, so you need a contract, and you should have a car." (The other women coaches didn't have cars as part of their compensation, I only wish I was *paid* like one of the guys!)

I don't know if these young girls in sports programs today know the pain of all the women who have gone before them, who wanted to do *exactly* what these young girls now get to do. Back then we weren't allowed to participate in certain things because "that's the way it's always been." So there was a whole generation of us who just climbed over the fence and played anyway, or went through windows and played anyway. I have stories for every level of all of this but my story is not what's important. What's important is that I see the spirit in these young kids and I don't want it squashed, I want it celebrated. I want to help them. For me it was to play sports. For someone else it might be to play in orchestra, it might be like Erin's niece, who wanted to do Pass, Punt, and Kick competition. Well hell, would I have loved to do that? So when I find out that she wins the *state* pass, punt, and kick, well, *you're a star!* I want a girl like this to talk to my classes and I want her to talk about what it was like. I want to celebrate this young girl who is a star.

Boys will be boys, that's fine, but let's allow girls to be *athletes*. Now the name-calling from "tomboy" becomes "athlete" and that's something that everybody can acknowledge and celebrate, *that's* what I'm excited about. (See Gaby's story further in the book.) These young girls can do these things and feel good about themselves, whereas I used to get scolded by my mother: "I don't know what you're trying to do," she'd say, "you're winning all of these things and why are you in all the boys' contests and why are you competing with all the boys?"

"Mom, they don't have it for girls," I said.

"Well jeepers, I go through town and I don't want people to think I have *five sons*."

I changed my name when I competed from Christine to Chris, and Chris was like the tiger on the court—I was going to play to win! My mother was always worried about the ribbon in my hair—well, heck, I just want to win the cup! I didn't care about how I looked. She was very into that because that's how she was brought up. There's a whole code that she taught me growing up. For instance, she would say to me all the time, "Ladies never run."

"C'mon, ma," I'd say, "ladies are always in high heels—how could they run?"

She'd say, "What am I going to do with you?" And this was a microcosm of our relationship throughout my childhood: "Ladies don't climb trees!"

"Well," I'd say, "I'm only eight years old!"

"Get out of the tree. I don't want people to see you."

But I was happy in the tree. "The other kids climb trees, why can't I climb with them?"

So whether it's climbing the tree or becoming an engineer or a chemist, *why not girls too*? But I was the outlier, I was the "Okay, you're a female, so . . ." You'd go see a guidance counselor and they'd say, "What do you want to be, a nurse, a teacher, or a secretary?"

"I want to be a physical educator," I'd say.

"No you don't," they'd say. "We don't want you to do that—you're too smart for that," and I was like *what the heck does that mean?*

"Why can't I help other girls play sports?" I asked.

"Oh Chris, this is the real world now. This isn't high school anymore." And there was just something in my spirit that I knew things had to change. I didn't think there was anything wrong with it. Luckily my dad was very supportive because he wanted somebody to play catch with, but my mom wasn't too thrilled. But I think in the end, when I was a college coach and a college administrator, she was very proud of that. And I think in her own quiet way, she was very proud of my successes in sports, in making my High School Hall of Fame and all of that, but I think she was just as proud of things that were more "traditionally female"—let's put it that way.

Sometimes you have to know the past in order to best visualize a future, and I think maybe there are moms now who are younger, who don't understand the passion that some moms have, moms who played college sports, who now want to make sure that they have good coaches and equipment for their daughters, and that their daughters are supported in a really positive way.

I've coached at so many different levels, from high school and junior high, to college and AAU[4]. I remember in AAU there was this young male coach, this big guy, and he's being Mr. Macho and he is just *blazing* comments at these young girls, like screaming at them. And here I am, and he doesn't know that I have 19 years college coaching experience and coached for years at the high school level, and he was an "ignorant person," we'll say, *screaming* at these girls that were sophomores and juniors in high school—I mean *screaming* in a game, in a summer league AAU game. I called a time out. I walked over to him and I said, "I'd like to talk to you for a minute."

"What?" he asked.

And this, I guess, is that boldness that my mom saw in me as a young girl. "I cannot be part of a game," I said, "where you're going to talk to your players like this."

"*Excuse* me?"

"They're young women," I said. "You shouldn't be talking to them like that. I'm a coach—I'm as competitive as anybody—but I'm giving them *specific* information. You know, 'Cut into the high post,' or 'Look to go back door.' Give them *directions*. But you are just standing here and

---

[4] Amateur Athletic Union, https://www.aausports.org/

criticizing them, like 'Stupid idiot! Oh that was so dumb! I can't believe you did that, that was so stupid! Did I say to do that?' You're just screaming at them. You really have to think about what you're saying to these young girls because someday they are going to grow up, and that is not the way you would want them to talk to *your daughter*."

He looked at me like, *Who the heck are you?*

Well here's the interesting part. After that game the parents of my players saw the parents of the other team come over to me and my girls' parents kind of hung around, ready for a problem. And when the game ended this other coach didn't even want to shake my hand. When it was over he walked by me and I said to him, "You better think about what kind of role model you want to be for these young girls." He looked at me like *Who the hell are you?*

But some of his girls' parents had come over and they said to me, "Wow. We wish our daughter played for you."

I said to them, "He doesn't understand that I've been the player out on that court. I know those girls want to play as well as they can—they want to play as hard as they can—but they need good coaching. They don't need people publicly putting them down. They don't need anybody embarrassing them. What they need is someone to *inspire* them. What they need are people who believe in them and who encourage them. *That's* why I'm doing this."

Over the years I've had a lot of players, and a lot of players became coaches. Some of my own assistant coaches have gone on to become head coaches at high schools and at colleges. One of my former players from the AAU who is now a college coach came to me and said, "Coach, I know you're retired, but I really, really need you! This is a really great group of girls and *they* really need you, and they need you for more than just basketball."

I didn't know what she meant at first but I eventually agreed, I said, "All right, all right, I'll take the team." Well I then saw, in the 21st century, how different it is, and why she wanted those young players exposed to my philosophy. She felt that I was very instrumental in her being a successful college player at the University of Maine, and in her opportunity to become the college coach she is today. She knows it's more than just how you dribble and handle the ball, that it has everything to do with how you think about yourself, and how you're going to deal with people that put roadblocks in your way, and how you're going to respond to those situations.

Everybody wants their kids to play sports, but they need to consider who the leaders of those girls will be. That makes such a difference—who they are and what they believe in. It's the coaches who will be around those girls every day, all day, or at practice for two hours each day. Those girls are going to hear their thoughts, they are going to hear their philosophy, and you want it to be a positive experience for the girls because they're putting their hearts and souls into it. So you want somebody as a coach who has a principled leadership style, and not one based simply on ego, on winning alone. There is so much more to it than that. So I think *Girl Power* is a book that should be read by men *and* women, and I wonder if guys will pick it up—I hope they do, I think that would be awesome. I hope people pick this book up whether they are in Boy Scouts, Girl Scouts, if they are in sports—anywhere the kids are developing their mindset it would be helpful. And I think for parents it can be pivotal.

I have a brother and we paralleled in the sports we played. He was the point guard and I was a forward; I played in college and he played in college. My team in high school had won the Eastern Massachusetts championship and his team finally made it to the state level his senior year. When his team won, the bishop of Fall River saw to it that the boys had a day out of school; they had a parade; they had a bus; they had all kinds of gifts. Well, we girls got nothing. The boys in my high school had *made it* to the state tournament (and ultimately lost). They got a letter from the bishop telling them how great they were. I was like, "All they did was play in it—we *won it!*" But we didn't get a letter from the bishop and that used to irritate me. I would argue this with the nuns, the principal, and the athletic director.

"How can you tell us we are all created in the image of God and we're all God's children? I don't think God would just be supportive of the boys and not the girls. Give us a shot! Let us have more practice time."

"Well," they'd say, "that's not the way it's *been*."

"Then it's got to change, because this isn't right," I said.

They say you make your plans and God laughs. Well, my brother, who gave me such a hard time growing up (we used to play the boys all the time and beat them!) now has four daughters—he never had a son. And boy, has his thought process changed completely! Now he looks at life very differently.

"Now I know why you were so angry," he told me. "Now I understand!" But I remember when his wife was pregnant for the first time and he said to me, "I hope it's a son. I want to play ball with him; I want to shoot hoops with him."

"And you're telling this to *me*? Richard," I said. "You better do that whether you have a son *or a daughter*. You do that with your *child*." He says that to this day he remembers that conversation, that it was like a slap across the face.

"And I said that to *you*, of all people!" he said.

"Hey," I said to him, "that's all I wanted, was to have someone play catch with me, to rebound for me, someone to play ball with."

We are all older and more mature now, and we can see it for what it is. I see it now as a process we had to go through. I think there were times, as a child, I was angry, I was frustrated, and I didn't know what to do. And there were no older women that could say, "Slow down—we'll help you." There was nobody to look to. So hopefully this will be like a game plan for a young girl who wants to exceed even her own expectations, and allow for other people to support her in that growth and development. There are times when you lose your confidence in yourself, as a girl, and hopefully that will change. *Girl Power* is about raising these girls up and celebrating them, it's about finding their uniqueness and their own excellence. I want to support that in any way I can.

—CHRISTINE BASILE

MAY 2, 2016

HOPKINTON, MASSACHUSETTS

INTRODUCTION

by ERIN MAHONEY, CREATOR of GIRL POWER

GIRL POWER WAS BORN about seven years ago. My niece was a first grader and she was being teased on the bus. Now, I do health and wellness, I'm a fitness gal. I also served in the military and I grew up in a house with a single mom and one sister. Hence the term *Girl Power*. I like to teach girls that they can be courageous and brave, that they can take care of themselves and still be kind and caring. And this is how the whole thing kind of came about. I thought, *How can I help Gaby (my niece) to not let these girls tease her and to feel like she can get on that bus?* Because at that point she didn't want to take the bus anymore. They were making fun of her clothes—kids can sometimes be mean—and they were calling her a tomboy, which isn't a terribly awful name, but she didn't like it. She was an athlete and she liked to wear a lot of sports things— New England Patriots, Red Sox—we New Englanders like to show our colors. My sister told her daughter Gaby to be brave and simply ask these girls to stop. "Tell them you don't like it when they call you a tomboy," she said. Gaby was shy but she found the courage and she asked them to stop. Unfortunately they continued so we needed to figure out a way to help Gaby get back on that bus.

My sister reached out to me, so I went on a mission and I found Gaby a t-shirt that said, "I am not a tomboy, I am an athlete," and everything changed. To see this little girl put something on that made her feel so empowered was amazing and you know what? You can put it back on others but still be kind and caring! She was taking care of herself and she really didn't have to say a thing—not a word. Suddenly those girls couldn't tease or hurt her feelings anymore. Something inside of me sparked in that moment. The fire inside of me was lit and I said to myself, *I know there are thousands of girls out there like Gabrielle, girls that might not know exactly how to handle a situation where they are being teased or feel left out. What can we do to empower girls and help them to feel confident and brave?*

I started developing this program that turned into eight classes. Each class has a topic/life lesson, an activity that connects to the topic, and a fitness segment. I love all things fitness, health, and wellness. I think it's important to give girls tools to take care of themselves both emotionally and physically. So I took life lessons, life skills, and fitness, and put them together. That grew into eight primary classes.

Before long a reporter got wind of what was happening with Girl Power, called me and said, "Can I come to your house and do an interview and see you in your office?" I was blown away. Over my desk in my office I have a little sign that says "Nothing great was ever achieved without enthusiasm." All over my office I have words like "Faith, Family, Dream, Believe, Imagine." He took a picture of me at my desk with the sign on my lap. That was really the first time I felt like this "Girl Power" thing was going to happen. It was going to reach lots of girls. When the article came out we were on the map! My niece Gaby was so cute. She was so little and so excited, and she was like a little celebrity. She was like, "Yeah, girls don't mess with me anymore—that's my auntie and she created Girl Power."

In fact, I was teaching in a school just this winter and Gaby and my sister came in to say hello. "Oh my gosh, Gabrielle, come in!" I introduced the girls and I said, "Girls this is Gabrielle, and she, Gaby, was the inspiration for the program!" They were so cute. They wanted her to sign their papers and she was like a little celebrity all over again. Maybe I'm crazy but I visualize her doing things in the Girl Power arena someday. Maybe we'll do workshops and she can be there saying "This made me feel like I didn't have to worry anymore, like I could be brave and courageous while being kind and caring!" She navigates relationships really well nowadays. Not that she doesn't have conflicts but I think she practices all the Girl Power tools. And these are the kinds of things I'd love to get across to girls all over the world.

I love when I read a book and it's *real*. I have a girlfriend who just became a social worker and she's in that counselor environment now, but I'll never forget when she was a mom of a girl who was in my program and she asked if I would be part of her thesis. She had to research organizations that make a difference and have an impact. I was so flattered, I said, "Oh my gosh, sure! That would be great!" So we gave her t-shirts and did an interview. She said when all of her grad school classmates graduate they all want to bring the Girl Power program to their schools. They think it's amazing, so I said, "Sure, let's do that, let's bring this program *everywhere*!" The response has been just phenomenal, and if we do things right it could be just crazy-amazing.

Another girlfriend of mine knew what I was doing when Girl Power was pretty much in its infancy, in the first twelve months. She gave me a great opportunity and she said, "Will you speak to all the Girl Scouts?" Well, little did I know that when I walked into the auditorium that there were about 300 Girl Scouts there and all of their parents! Now, I am a fly-by-the-seat-of-my-pants girl. I didn't really have anything written down, it was just going to be something quick. So I went up there and I started talking to all the girls. I had them all get up on their feet and do "I am" statements, and had them say, "I am strong! I am beautiful, I am kind, I am amazing!" It was so loud! It was so crazy, the energy we were able to stir up was over the top. It was partly because I was like, *Oh my gosh, what are we going to do here?* So I did what I do in the gym. I kind of pretended the parents weren't there and I just focused on the girls. It was so much fun. As they repeat, "I am strong, I am beautiful, I am powerful," I then say, "Yes, you are. Don't let anyone tell you different!" It was *just awesome.* And of course the parents wanted to know how and where they could get more of this for their girls.

After that event my sister and I talked about how I might take Girl Power to the next level, to reach more girls. She was very active in the local PTA and suggested that I put something together on paper and submit it as an after school program. Well, thank you Michelle! Your brilliant idea and belief in me helped us take this program to girls in the afterschool programming, to parks and recreations, and have a larger presence in Girl Scouts all over Massachusetts! I didn't always listen to my big sister but I'm sure glad I did that day.

As the program developed I wasn't sure if this project would end up as eight small books or one primary book, but I needed to train instructors. Girl Power had by that time quickly spread to *eighteen* towns and I could not teach all those classes myself, I have a family I'm raising two kids (all boys, ironically). So I needed to create a manual so I could *train the trainer*. It took about two years for the manual and another year for the book you now hold along with the *Girl Power Journal* for girls.

This book is my vehicle to get my work and this amazing empowerment program out to the world! We've had bumps in the road along the way but all were great opportunities to learn, to improve, and to teach others about the message and mission of Girl Power, empowering girls! Part of my vision was to have this sweet little book where young girls—whether they be in the first grade or middle school—can be reading these books before bed feeling empowered, reminded of how strong, smart, and amazing they are before drifting off to sleep.

So imagine now, that we have these books! We can hold a two-hour workshop and have these books available. Or perhaps a Girl Scout leader on the West Coast wants to teach Girl Power to her troop. The books bring the program to everyone everywhere! For thousands of moms or dads who want to help their daughters who might be struggling with friends—maybe their daughter isn't a great eater; maybe their daughter doesn't get enough rest or lacks confidence, whatever they are having issues with—we can provide insight, activities, and proven strategies in these books to help. I would love to be that gal—able to reach thousands of girls and tell them, "*You* have the *power* to *rock the day!* Love yourself, do your best, and choose happy!"

So this is *so* exciting, and this is my vision, that girls all over the globe can now learn the Girl Power principles and lessons. She can build confidence and strength. She can grow into her best self! If a girl has a crummy day at school or they have a fight on the bus with a girlfriend—and girls can be mean—they will know what to do in such a way that even the bully is spared. The foundation of good health for adults and kids, boys and girls, men and women, I teach my girls. I tell them to *stand in your light, stand in your power.* I think it's something that people don't hear or get everywhere. I teach these lessons and this program wherever I can but with books I'm now able to share *Girl Power* with the world.

I hope you thoroughly enjoy *Girl Power* and get great use out of this guidebook and the accompanying workbook for girls. I know that these principles and activities can help girls develop into what they are *all* meant to be—*strong, smart,* and *amazing!*

A NOTE TO READERS

by RODNEY MILES

THE *GIRL POWER GUIDEBOOK* and the *Girl Power Journal* were designed to work together, but in making each individual volume as clear and effective as they can be on their own, there are some slight differences. For example, what we call "classes" in this guidebook are called "steps" in the workbook. This is so girls doing Girl Power on their own or not exactly according to an eight-week program can still feel 100 percent included, and find and embrace their own *Girl Power* at their own convenience and pace.

The *Girl Power Journal* is designed for any girl to simply go though, page by page, step by step, and we've included all worksheets and exercises right there, in the journal/workbook, even up to a graduation certificate that can be removed and filled in for each girl, and beyond, into several appendices which we think are fun and nice additions for the girls, like a photo album and places for notes. It's also beautifully illustrated by artist Keith Seidel!

The book you now hold, the *Girl Power Guidebook,* was intended as an aid to parents and instructors for greater understanding and delivery. In it, you'll find all of the steps the girls take in the *Journal,* and these are all the steps they take in the eight-week or eight-step Girl Power program. These steps are listed out and described at the beginning of each chapter, under the heading, "Class Organization and Materials," and a separate chapter is devoted to each class. After the program steps in each chapter you'll find a section called, "Background and Theory," which is an informal discussion by Erin, describing what to expect in certain classes, common questions and reactions girls seem to have, ways to handle the girls positively in each setting, the origin and history of some of the Girl Power steps, and a lot more. And certain aspects of this guidebook are self-explanatory (we hope!). For example, when you see content in quotes, it is usually intended as dialogue to be said to the girls as opposed to simply internal notes or thoughts for you as an instructor.

The language (and writing) used throughout both *Girl Power* books intentionally preserves Erin's voice. It's casual and conversational. It's energetic and not just hopeful, but positively confident. The hope is to provide a reading experience that I believe *greatly* enhances a reader's understanding of why and how Erin has made Girl Power such a success. When you talk to Erin, and when she explains the things she does in Girl Power and why, so much more comes through than simple instructions and rationale. Her passion, for one, her positivity, for another, and her magical way of communicating with an eight-to-thirteen-year-old girl that one can easily imagine is happily received by said girl. She talks to her Girl Power Girls like they would like and deserve to be talked to, as *powerful, good, intelligent, positive* human beings. So it's no surprise to me that this is the effect she has on her girls. I wanted, as a writer, to share that with the world, just as much as the details. Our honest expectations of people, and *how* we say things, influence them even more than what is said. Erin *knows* how powerful girls are, and that comes through in her voice.

It's the author's (and her team's) *dream* to see more and more girls being empowered to live positive, happy lives in their own power at a young age, and every effort has been made to make these books not only useful and complete, but fun and exciting as well! Your feedback and involvement with the larger Girl Power program is *always welcome*. Please do enjoy your time and your child's experience in and with *Girl Power*, and please tell us about it! Also be sure to visit www.GirlPowerGo.com and sign up for email updates as the Girl Power program is committed to being vibrant, dynamic, and always growing into a larger and larger movement, and we want you to be a part, big or small.

Be strong! Be smart! Be amazing!

CLASS #1: WELCOME AND INTRODUCTION TO GIRL POWER

IN THIS CHAPTER

CLASS ORGANIZATION
AND MATERIALS

BACKGROUND
AND THEORY

- Part 1: Welcome and Warm Up
- Part 2: Activity
- Part 3: Fitness
- Part 4: Wrap Up
- Equipment and Materials
- Welcome Letter
- Positive Thoughts

- Excitement and Fear
- Hearts and Minds
- Empowering Girls
- Self-Portraits
- Common Ground

CLASS ORGANIZATION AND MATERIALS

PART 1: WELCOME AND WARM UP

<u>Get the Group Moving:</u> Have the group spread out and warm up with dynamic stretching[5], jumping jacks, running in place or laps around the room, and then with static stretching[6]. Do this for three to five minutes to warm up and help them burn some nervous/excited energy. Then call the group to sit in front of you.

<u>Welcome All the Girls to Class:</u> Introduce yourself and give a little background on what you do. Let them know something interesting and fun about yourself and why you are excited to be part of Girl Power.

---

[5] Dynamic stretching is a form of stretching beneficial in sports utilizing momentum from form, and the momentum from static-active stretching strength, in an effort to propel the muscle into an extended range of motion not exceeding one's static-passive stretching ability.
(https://en.wikipedia.org/wiki/Dynamic_stretching)

[6] Static stretching is used to stretch muscles while the body is at rest. It is composed of various techniques that gradually lengthen a muscle to an elongated position (to the point of discomfort) and hold that position for 30 seconds to two minutes.
(https://en.wikipedia.org/wiki/Static_stretching)

Introduce Girl Power: For example: "Girl Power was designed to get girls excited about being strong, independent, self-confident and healthy! Over the next several weeks, you will be given tools to make good friends, make healthy food choices, feel fabulous about yourself and your body, and all while having fun. You will learn life skills that will serve you well in class, with friends, with family, in sports, and in every aspect of your life."

Have the Girls Introduce Themselves: Have them share their name, something they love to do, a favorite thing, or something interesting about themselves. Prompt questions if they're shy, for example, "What's your favorite color? How did you hear about the class? What's your pet's name?" and so on.

Introduce "I Am" Statements: Tell the girls that throughout the class everyone will be *shouting* different "I Am" statements from time to time to remind them all of how fabulous they are. Start with an example: "I Am Smart!" Let the group know that it is time for the "I Am" statement and ask them to chant as loudly as they can in three seconds. Count down "three, two, one," and have them yell the statement. Use statements like, "I am strong, I am amazing, I am fabulous, I am kind, I am beautiful," and so on. You can ask for their ideas to include as well. Every once in a while tell them "Yes, you are! Don't let anyone tell you different" after their "I Am" statement!

PART 2: ACTIVITY

<u>Paper and Self-Portrait Activity:</u> Direct the girls to the self-portrait sheet in their journals/workbooks (or hand out individual sheets). Have them spread out on the floor. Open the bin of markers and colored pencils and ask each girl to draw a picture of themselves on the sheet. Encourage them to use as many colors as they would like and then leave them to create (as this will be very important later). Let the girls share their pictures with the rest of the group if they would like to. Have them all help pick up the supplies as they are finished. Collect all the pictures when they are completed and save them in a safe place.

PART 3: FITNESS

<u>Mini Boot Camp:</u> Set up a mini boot camp consisting of different exercise stations for the girls to go through.

Set up:

- one station with jump ropes,
- one with a cone zigzag course,
- and one with hula hoops.

Demonstrate what they will be doing at each station. Have them stay at each station for one full minute then switch to the next. They can go through each two to three times, depending on time left in class.

Insert "I Am" Statements: This is a good time to include a couple more "I Am" statements. You can't do too many "I Am" statements during class because this reinforces positive self-thoughts. Ask for volunteers to come up with words to use. Examples include "smart, brave, fabulous, and amazing." In fact, while administering Girl Power, do "I Am" statements whenever you need to redirect. This is a great tool for keeping the girls focused on the activity or fitness you are teaching.

Clean Up: Have the group help pick up all the equipment.

PART 4: WRAP UP

Class Commencement: Have the girls come back together in a group. Give them some positive feedback from the class. Verbally assign them any homework that they should do over the week.

Greet Parents: Greet the parents as they come for pick-up and answer any questions they have. Positive energy and friendliness go a long way!

EQUIPMENT AND MATERIALS

- Jump ropes
- Hula hoops

- Flat, round cones
- Self-portrait blank pages
- Bin of markers and colored pencils

WELCOME LETTER

You can use the following letter, either provided in print or by email ideally prior to the first class, or at the time of the first class:

Welcome Parents and Participants!!

I am very excited to have the opportunity to work with you over the next several weeks! I guarantee it will be fun, inspiring, thought-provoking, and challenging all at the same time. The following are a few things you should have for each class to make it a great experience:

- *Comfortable gym clothes*
- *Sneakers*
- *A water bottle*
- *A positive attitude*
- *A smile* ☺

Bring those things and I will bring the rest!

Make it an amazing day!

(Sign your name)

POSITIVE THOUGHTS

FOR THE WEEK AND BEYOND!

Positive thoughts should be repeated and shouted out by the girls often—definitely at this point in the class but also whenever seems like an opportune time to do them. Simply announce, "Ready for some positive thoughts? Okay! Three, two, one . . ."

Tell the girls to read these positive thoughts every night before bed (they have them in their workbooks) and every morning before their feet hit the floor! Positive thoughts have been supplied for the most part, but you and your Girl Power girls are free to make up and say your own, of course!

I can do ANYTHING
I set my mind to!

I am AMAZING
just the way I am!

BACKGROUND AND THEORY

EXCITEMENT AND FEAR

SOMETIMES YOU MIGHT have girls in your class that kind of exude a certain kind of "confidence," like they have to take over the room, but often those that "take over the room" or require a lot of attention also have trouble sharing the spotlight because they in reality *lack* self-confidence, and the boldness they display is often a front. I help girls to see that it's okay to calm down, and there's power in listening to others, to help them see that you can learn a lot about other people by listening, and that can go back and forth. Once they truly experience that, it can be a life-changer, and girls can become more interested in others while becoming more relaxed about themselves. You can share conversations rather than taking over or filling the entire room with your personality.

This I know because I sometimes *am* that girl. I come in like a stick of dynamite full of energy and ready to rock it! I need at times to remind myself to slow down and access the audience. All that energy, although positive, can be intimidating, and sometimes people can't keep up. Sometimes you can lose an audience that way. I tell the girls to be themselves as well as being thoughtful and considerate of others. When you have such important things to say it's important to slow down a little bit, and say things in a way that exudes confidence *and* calm. I have them practice taking turns speaking so they can each go at their own pace. There are always girls that are a little more shy or quiet, and I'm always making sure they don't get squeezed out of the discussion.

Sometimes in the first class we talk about excitement, after we talk about the course a little bit, and then we talk about fear. For example, some girls don't view themselves as athletic, so that can stir up a little fear: "I'm nervous about the fitness, Mrs. Mahoney," they might say. Some girls are struggling with their weight—maybe they don't feel very fit. But a lot of the girls are afraid of the same thing. Lily looks at Linda and thinks Linda always looks super put-together. Well, it sometimes happens that Linda's thinking the same thing about Lily! Yet the two girls are both feeling somewhat insecure and nervous. Girl Power allows them to share these feelings and realize in a beautiful way that although they are each unique and special, they are actually more alike than they might have ever imagined.

HEARTS AND MINDS

So getting them to open their minds and their hearts is sometimes a very tricky piece of this program.. I tell the girls "Nothing awesome comes out of a comfort zone." Safe places get boring fast, meaning I encourage girls to be fearless, and teach them that when you move out of that comfort zone or safe place you then have the opportunity to shine and be brave in a whole new way. You move into that slightly scary place where your belly is doing flips. It's *that* place where awesome things can happen.

For example, when you don't think you can run any farther but you decide to push yourself a little harder and just

19

like magic you find you are still running! Or, when you don't think that you can invite that girl that's kind of a stranger to sit at the lunch table with you, but you do, and you see the happiness on her face! When you push yourself to do the things that make you feel scared or afraid, unsure or downright terrified, you often experience great joy and feelings of success or accomplishment. It also opens the door for girls to feel proud of themselves and it's rare that people ever have regrets doing this. Go BIG or go home, as they say!

It's rare that people move out of their comfort zones without help. I tell the girls that they can and in fact should move out of their comfort zones as often as possible! Nothing amazing happens in a comfort zone, anyway. Getting the girls to move out of their comfort zones builds confidence. It allows them to challenge themselves in new ways. I tell them that the comfort zone or "comfortable" is just too slow, boring at times and certainly not exciting! I tell them to go to the place where they think they're slightly terrified or where they might even get sick and GO THERE, DO THAT, and then be like, "Oh man, I just did that!"

Initially I may need to give the girls a gentle push out of their comfort zone. One of the ways I might do this is to place the girls in groups if we're doing an activity where they have to work together. I ask what their birth month is and group them by that, because I'll often get the girls who try to stick with other girls they already know. They might rush over to their little group of friends right away because they are not comfortable or open to working with girls they don't know well (or know at all yet). See, if I line them up against the wall, and I have them call off numbers like "one, two, three, four," by the end of the line they will figure out, "If I'm a number two I'll get to be with my girlfriends." So instead, I ask them when their birthdays are, and I separate them by birth month. I may put May, August, and September together, for example. By the time they figure out what's happening, it's done. But that's just one example of how I push them out of their safe place. We then do a team activity. Sometimes it's a physical activity and sometimes it's something they have to work through.

I try to get each girl at some point in the eight weeks, in some way, shape, or form, to actually stand up and speak in front of the class, which can be very scary, and we talk about that. It's also very empowering for the girls to share things about themselves. We have a worksheet that they do which includes, among other things, "Things I Love About Me." I'll ask who wants to share, and I'll definitely kind of focus on who might not be comfortable sharing in the beginning, trying to just gently encourage them to share by the end of class, or whenever they feel ready. They can share one sentence or they can share the whole piece (it's usually about five different things).

So those are just a few ways that I can gently push them out of their comfort zones. They might not realize what's happening but they become very empowered by these activities. By sharing of themselves and listening to each other they have an opportunity to grow, feel safe, and perhaps try new things. The key is to teach girls how to accept their differences, embrace their similarities, and not judge anything in between.

The girls I work with have different talents and interests, different family dynamics, similar likes and dislikes, and have their own learning styles—which become their own ways to learn from one another. But they soon find there is comfort in knowing that they are all unique and similar in many ways. Out of the hundreds of classes I've given and thousands of girls I have worked with, I always learn new things from them each and every time I teach. And while things are always changing, so many of the "hot topics" seem to remain the same—navigating relationships with friends, parents and teachers; our relationship with ourselves; practicing love and kindness; being brave and courageous; practicing positive, healthy self-care and proper rest and nutrition; social media or the problem with "three" when it comes to friends, and the list goes on. It has evolved in large part into the Girl Power program, so we are addressing vital subjects for these young girls.

EMPOWERING GIRLS

So two huge factors in empowering young girls is to help them feel confident and to build mutual trust. Often in the first class the girls really don't know what they signed up for. So this is a time when we can start to meet each other and share a little bit about ourselves. It's an introduction period of me to them, them to me, them to each other, and them to the Girl Power program. We need to learn what the girls' personalities are, what their likes are, what their dislikes are, so I take time to tell the girls a little bit about the program, how it came about and a little bit about me and my background. Then it's their turn to introduce themselves to each other. The girls don't always come from the same school. Some girls come bravely into the first class without knowing anyone. Other times most of the girls know each other. Either way it's a time of uncertainty as well as excitement, of course.

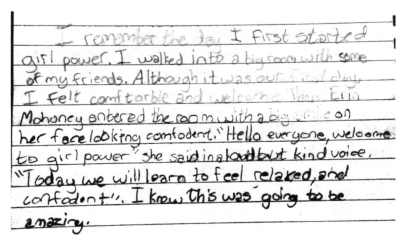

I remember the day I first started girl power. I walked into a big room with some of my friends. Although it was our first day, I felt comftorble and welcome. Then Erin Mohoney entered the room with a big smile on her face looking comfodent. "Hello everyone, welcome to girl power" she said in a loud but kind voice, "Today we will learn to feel relaxed, and confodent". I know this was going to be amazing.

And it's in this first class that the single most important thing is to get them to realize that we're going to do a lot of discovery—we'll be helping them to discover a lot of things about themselves and each other—and to let them know what the purpose of the Girl Power program is (to empower them!). They will learn how to take good care of themselves, learn good love and kindness practices, learn a little bit about nutrition, and among other things learn to be powerful and happy. I tell them how classes will work and flow, and that we're going to have some fun while we learn some great tools and life lessons. Every class will have a topic, a fitness segment, and an activity that relates to the topic. Sometimes we do teamwork things, sometimes we do individual activities, and in every class we have discussions and share. It's an opportunity for them to ask questions (and I ask questions of them as well). It's the best way for us to learn by interacting in a way that is fun, accepting, kind, loving, and respectful.

We discuss how we need to let everyone speak and that no one needs to share if they don't feel comfortable, at least in the first class. I have found that even the shyest girls want to share and become very comfortable in this setting by about Class 3. I'll ask the older girls, in a kidding way, "Who's here because you wanted to take Girl Power?" Very few hands go up. Then I'll ask them, "Who's here because your mom or your dad made you come?" Most hands go up. We share a giggle because it's funny! Then I tell them that I love a challenge. I also tell them that "it's not my first rodeo and I promise by Class 2 you will be psyched that you are here!" That usually allows us to connect in some small way right out of the gate. They realize that I'm a straight-shooter and they just might have fun, whether they want to or not! Girls in fifth and sixth grades, especially, are getting ready to approach middle school and they clearly know everything about everything and they don't feel that they need this class. So, guess what? We dig right in and we talk about that! You get the idea.

SELF-PORTRAITS

At the beginning of the eight-week program, in this first class, I have all the girls draw a self-portrait. At the top of the page it has their name and the date, the Girl Power logo and the tag line: "Be Strong, Be Smart, Be Amazing." The rest of the page is blank. I have had girls draw pictures that bring tears to my eyes. If you analyze self-portraits, it's really how kids see themselves (and even adults). This one particular girl drew herself so tiny—like the size of your thumbnail—and she had all these other things in the picture. She had a dog, she had some friends, she had some trees, but by the end of the eight weeks, she could not fit her head on the page! What that screams is that she came in and she felt like she needed support from her friends. She felt small and perhaps powerless—even her smile (she drew a straight line for her mouth) and in her picture after the eight weeks she drew her braces! It's amazing, it's crazy! Watching how girls change and transform in the program is hard to put into words. When this all began I'm not sure I even realized the impact and possibilities that would lie ahead.

So right from the beginning we begin to build trust and confidence, and that creates a safe place for the girls to be themselves. When they do their self-portraits in Week 1, I bring those self-portraits home and I study them. I look at every shape that they drew, every detail—how do their eyes look? And their mouth—are they smiling? Or is their mouth straight? Are they showing their teeth? I look at all of these things and more. What's the size of their body in their first self-portrait? Did they draw the whole person? Did they just draw just their head? Do they have other things in the picture such as friends, family, trees, or pets? Is the sun shining? Is it stormy or grey?

First class and last class self-portraits.

Self-portraits tell us so much about kids, about girls, even adults. When people draw or create a self-portrait from the heart without analysis or much thought it's pretty amazing what develops and what you can learn and/or interpret about the person from the picture. We do this exercise again in the last class (in the eighth week) at graduation. Week 8 has a time set aside for us to review and discuss how the girls have grown. We discuss what their favorite parts of the class were as well as their least favorite, and they then do their self-portrait again. So in this first class I collect the portraits and they don't see them again until the end of the eight weeks. At the end of the program if they want to keep them they can. Sometimes they will want me to keep them (which I love!). If I don't keep the portraits, I take pictures of them so we can learn from them. These portraits are evidence that transformation and growth is taking place. Girls build self-esteem, friendships grow, and they learn life skills that help them to navigate the many aspects of their own lives.

Doing self-portraits in the Girl Power program has an interesting origin. I actually struggled to read when I was younger. My mom put me in a program because I was having trouble and I felt stupid. It's funny now because that was my first exposure to the self-portrait. I was "that kid" a long, long time ago and that's why I incorporate this into my classes, because I know the impact it had on me. The head teacher or principal at this summer program sat me down in her office and I was very nervous. I was embarrassed to be in this class because I couldn't read very well. But my mom couldn't read very well either. She struggled her whole life and no one helped her, and she used to say to me, "I'm not going to let you struggle like I did." So the woman running the program had me draw a picture of myself and I really didn't understand it at the time.

Then we went through the summer—those six weeks—and did all these funky things. For example, they blindfold us and had us draw lines on the chalkboard. It was odd to me at the time. Turned out it was not just reading but reading *comprehension* and it focused me on listening more and paying attention to detail. It was very interesting. It was this great program! In the end she brought me back into the office and she had me draw my self-portrait again. I was probably in the first or second grade and I had totally forgotten that I had drawn a picture just weeks before. Then she took the previous picture out of her desk drawer and put the two side-by-side. And even at that young age I knew that something in me had changed. I knew that I was a *huge* person that last day of that silly reading program (that I at first never wanted to be a part of!). But what changed? My self-*confidence*, that's what! I was not afraid to be me anymore! I was terrified to read out loud my whole life up until then and in that magical moment the fear was gone!

And I'll never forget a pivotal moment later in my life that came as a result of that program I did when I was young. Maybe five or six years before my mother passed away, my cousin Jon got married and he asked me to *read* at his wedding. It was a very difficult piece of reading, but I was so completely honored that he would ask me to be part of his special day in that way, I knew I needed to do it. He didn't need to know I was slightly terrified (fears come back, you see) but I got up there and I read. I looked out at the wedding guests and I was very confident. I spoke slowly and clearly. I was very excited to be doing that for my cousin Jon, and when I got back into the pew and sat down next to my mother, I realized she was crying.

"What are you crying about?" I asked her.

"That was not a little girl up there who could not read," she said. And I'll never forget the look on her face or the love and pride in her eyes. It was one of the greatest moments that my mother and I ever shared.

We forget sometimes, how far we've come.

COMMON GROUND

Some of the girls do have huge transformations throughout the program, and they don't even know it's happening! I think it all kind of starts in that first class where they have to learn to trust me and what my intentions are. They're going to have an opportunity to discover some things that they don't even know they love yet. And maybe they'll begin a friendship with someone they see in school but who they don't really know yet. Maybe they're going to find a common interest with someone: "Oh, I didn't know you play the clarinet! I play the clarinet too, I just don't play it at school," for example. So just giving them that space and that time to be open-minded is so important, and you can't rush that process.

One of the ways I begin to build trust with the girls is I open up and tell them about myself a little bit. I tell them about my background and fears that I had as a young girl or as a teenager or young woman. I want them to know I'm "real," that I have been where they are. I then encourage them to share. Again, if I have very shy girls in class who don't want to say anything at first, I don't force them to. Later on in the program they might feel ready. But they get to listen to some of the things the other girls share—you know, "Do you have a pet? What's your favorite color? What do you like to do in your free time?" These are all things that make each person very special and very unique. These are also, of course, things that the girls may have in common. So right from the first class the girls learn that they have the power to impact others in a really positive way and I tell girls, "It's our responsibility to take care of each other and be kind and caring. If you see something happening that's not right or not kind and as long as you feel safe, meaning that this person is not going to hurt you in some way, then you address that with them right there. Stand up for those that can't stand up for themselves, and go that extra mile with a random act of kindness."

Class 1, first self-portraits.

In any case, whatever the issue is in a child's life at any given time, I've found that by bringing the issue to the classroom (without embarrassing the girl) it helps girls realize that many kids have not only the same likes and interests, but the same issues, fears, and insecurities. It's very interesting. Different things make them lack confidence. There's not a magical age where kids become comfortable with things that cause them fear like the dark, elevators, or sleepovers. There's not a magical age when all of the sudden everybody is comfortable with these things. Some kids never mind the dark or the rising of an elevator. Other kids—fifth, sixth, seventh grade—still don't love the dark very much, they just like the lights on better. We can help them to realize that's okay. They all grow and develop at different paces and it's okay not to like the same things as your friends.

~

Girl Power is all about teaching kids to help each other to feel confident and safe and to be open to moving out of their comfort zones. It's about them learning to like supporting each other, to embrace and accept their differences and always try their best to practice love and kindness. And it all starts in the first class.

CLASS #2: BRAVE AND COURAGEOUS, "WARRIOR CLASS"

IN THIS CHAPTER

CLASS ORGANIZATION AND MATERIALS

- Part 1: Welcome and Warm Up
- Part 2: Fitness
- Part 3: Activity
- Part 4: Fitness
- Part 5: Wrap Up
- Equipment and Materials
- Positive Thoughts

BACKGROUND AND THEORY

- Brave and Courageous
- Stand in Your Power
- Keeping Safe
- If You Teach Them, They Will Learn!

CLASS ORGANIZATION AND MATERIALS

PART 1: WELCOME AND WARM UP

<u>Get the Group Moving</u>: Have the group spread out and warm them up with dynamic stretching, jumping jacks, running in place or laps around the room, then static stretching. Do this for 3-5 minutes to warm them up and help them burn some nervous/excited energy. Then call the group to sit in front of you.

<u>Review Homework</u>: If homework was assigned the previous class, go over it together. Encourage the girls to share what they did that made them feel happy this week with the rest of the group.

<u>Discuss What it Means to be Brave and Courageous</u>: "Being brave and courageous means doing the right thing when no one else does, it means having the courage to stand up for what you feel is right, or it can be trying something new that you don't feel confident about at first. Bravery can be used in many situations."

Ask the girls to share an experience when they felt they had to be brave or courageous. Maybe it was going to a new school, trying a new sport, getting to know a new friend, trying a new food, or entering a room in the dark. Share one of your own experiences when you had to be brave and courageous. Talk about "warriors" and how they are brave and courageous, often entering scary or dangerous situations to defend something that is right or needs to be corrected or fixed.

Remind the girls that they should always first and foremost keep themselves safe. Being brave and courageous *and* smart is what Girl Power is all about. For example, if they see someone being picked on while on the playground or out at recess but the child that is doing the bullying is bigger and has many friends around him or her, they should not put themselves in danger. This is a situation when they could be brave and courageous by going to get help from an adult. If they feel safe, they could attempt to help the child themselves but must always use good judgment.

Inner and Outer Strength: Discuss how important it is for the girls to create both inner and outer strength. Inner strength examples include being kind, making good decisions, and practicing patience. Outer strength examples are being active by running and playing sports, and by cleaning up when you're done with projects.. Making good food choices that will fuel their bodies for strength and endurance would be an example of both inner and outer strength.

Standing Up for Themselves and Others: Discuss how girls can be brave and courageous by standing up for themselves and others in a kind and thoughtful way but while also being assertive when necessary.

Examples to Share and Discuss:

35

- "Third-girl-out" situations;
- When they see someone not being treated well;
- Seeing someone sitting alone at lunch.

Expand and add your own examples as they come up. The girls are normally happy to share their own experiences here, so be sure to listen carefully as they will be your future examples, and you will have more and more, the more you instruct Girl Power.

PART 2: FITNESS

Kickboxing Lesson: Have the girls spread out and explain the rules in a fun way, the first rule being that they are not allowed to use the moves on *each other or on their siblings*—that this is just for them!

Kickboxing Sequences to Teach: Start with *on-guard*, also called *warrior stance*: Feet are slightly wider than the shoulders. Hands are in a tight fist protecting the face with knuckles facing outward. Girls are in a slight squatted position and ready to defend or attack.

Instruct the Girls to Feel their Power. "YOU have the power to protect your house, yourself and your friends! Own it!" Demonstrate and have them repeat, practice, and feel the energy. Tell them to growl and let it out! They will follow your lead here so go after it with energy and conviction. "You are strong, brave and courageous!"

Begin with Basic Punches: Jab, cross punch, upper cuts and hook. Demonstrate each punch and then put them together:

- Jab: While in a warrior or on-guard stance, the lead fist is thrown straight ahead and the arm is fully extended. It is an overhand punch—at the moment of impact, the pronated[7] fist is generally held in a horizontal orientation with the palm facing the ground.
- Cross Punch: This punch is thrown by the rear hand. It literally crosses the body in a straight line prior to contact with the target.
- Upper Cut: While in a warrior stance, sweep your fist upward aiming at the invisible opponent's chin.
- Hook: This punch is performed by turning the core muscles and back, thereby swinging the arm, which is bent at an angle near or at 90 degrees, in a horizontal arc into the invisible opponent.

Move on to Kicks: Front kick, back kick, roundhouse kick. Again teach and demonstrate.

---

[7] pronate, turn or hold (a hand, foot, or limb) so that the palm or sole is facing downward or inward. (Google definition)

- <u>Front Kick</u>: A front kick is executed by lifting the knee straight forward while keeping the foot and shin either hanging freely or pulled to the hip, and then straightening the leg in front of you to strike the target area. Retract the leg immediately after delivering the kick.

- <u>Back Kick</u>: Also referred to as a donkey kick, mule kick, or turning back kick, this kick is directed backwards, keeping the kicking leg close to the standing leg and using the heel as a striking surface.

- <u>Roundhouse Kick</u>: Not to be confused with the round kick or turning kick, this is the most commonly used kick in kickboxing due to its power and ease of use. The instep is used to strike. To execute, the attacker swings their leg sideways in a circular motion, kicking the opponent's side with the top of their foot.

<u>Karate Punch:</u> Standing with toes pointing outward in a squat position, have the girls punch towards the floor twisting on the way back up. Punch with power, pull back in with confidence! Then faster, like you mean it!

Recovery Moves[8]:

- Shuffle in place.
- Speed bag with quarter-turns around the room or in place. Start with one hand, then the other, and then put it together.
- Jack it out ("Jumping Jill's").
- Jack with a punch.
- Bob and weave.
- Jab towards the floor and over-head punch in place, left and right sides.

Speed Moves[9]: These really increase the intensity and heart rate:

- Football shuffle left and right if space allows, or in place if using a smaller space or have a very large class.
- Flurry with upper cuts as fast as you can while in a squatting position.
- High knees.

[ ] Recovery moves are moves that allow you to catch your breath. They are a little slower and require less energy than speed moves. Recovery moves are also used to transition or change from one movement (like a punch or kick) to another.

[ ] Speed moves increase your heart rate, burn more calories and energy and make you fierce. It's important to sprinkle both recovery and speed moves into your training! Speed moves really increase our Girl Power because they are so intense!

You may sequence the punches, kicks, recovery and speed moves any way that you would like, just be sure that your transitions are safe. Use marching in between when making position changes and keep it basic.

Add in "I Am" statements throughout, such as "I am brave! I am courageous! I am strong! I am powerful! I am kind! I am smart! I am awesome!" and so on.

PART 3: ACTIVITY

Face Paint – Warrior Paint: Explain the rules before you hand out the face paint crayons:

- The girls should only paint their faces, not their bodies. They can paint whatever they feel they want their warrior to show or look like.
- Ask if any of them need to be somewhere right after class that would prevent them from being able to paint their face.
- Double check to see if anyone has allergies to face paint or dyes that would prevent them from using them.

Girls that don't want to turn into warriors with the face painting crayons can help their friends or be active with a jump rope. They could also draw a picture of what they think a warrior might look like or the Girl Power superhero or characters.

Set Up: Set up as many stations as you need using long mirrors. These can be leaned up against a wall or other safe spot so that the girls can lie on the floor in front of them. Place paper towels down for them to put the face paint crayons on. This keeps the floor or work surface clean.

Remind them that warriors are brave and courageous and stand up for what is right, that they do the right thing when no one else does. Hand out the face paint crayons and let them go! Make sure they are using them appropriately and offer help if they need it. They often just naturally help each other, which is a great way for the group to come together early in the program.

Insert "I Am" Statements: This is another good time to include a couple more "I Am" statements. Ask for volunteers to come up with words to use. "I am powerful! I am fearless! I am brave! I am courageous!" is a great start.

Clean Up: Have the group help pick up all the supplies. Hand out the hand wipes if they need/want to clean off any of the face paint.

PART 4: FITNESS

Review Kickboxing: Have the girls spread out and assume their warrior or on-guard stance. Run through the routine you practiced earlier.

Include "I Am" statements! Now that they are all in warrior paint, this is the best time to let them feel the power of being warriors! Remind the girls that they are fabulous and *don't let anyone tell them different*! Own it and choose to be awesome!

PART 5: WRAP UP

<u>Class Commencement:</u> Have the girls come back together in a group. Give them some positive feedback from the class. Remind them to make good decisions and to be brave and courageous. Hand out more wipes as they leave just in case they need to clean off their faces. Otherwise it's always fun to let them go home as warriors!

<u>Verbally Assign Homework:</u> Tell the girls to continue to do something every day that makes them feel happy, brave, or courageous. Challenge them to do all three this week!

<u>Greet Parents:</u> Greet the parents as they come for pick-up and answer any questions they have. Positive energy and friendliness go a long way!

EQUIPMENT AND MATERIALS

- 3 long mirrors
- 2 rolls paper towels
- 2 containers of face wipes
- Face paint crayons

- Paper for girls that may not be painting faces
- Marker and colored pencil bin

POSITIVE THOUGHTS

FOR THE WEEK AND BEYOND!

Continue to do ONE thing every day that makes you HAPPY!

I Am BRAVE and COURAGEOUS!

I CHOOSE to be AWESOME!

BACKGROUND AND THEORY

Applying "warrior paint" in the Brave and Courageous class.

BRAVE AND COURAGEOUS

BEING BRAVE AND COURAGEOUS means doing the right thing when no one else does; it means having the courage to stand up for what you feel is right, or trying something new that you don't feel confident about. Bravery can be used in many situations. At times I have the girls share an experience when they felt they had to be brave or courageous. I then share some of my own experiences when I had to be brave and courageous. We talk about being "warriors" and how they are brave and courageous, often entering scary or dangerous situations to defend something that is right or needs to be corrected or fixed. I talk with the girls and teach them the importance of developing both inner and outer strength. Inner strength examples include being kind, making good decisions, and practicing patience. Outer strength examples are being active by running, dancing, playing with friends, or playing sports.

And it's important to understand that girls can be brave and courageous by standing up for themselves and others *in a kind and thoughtful way* but while also being assertive when necessary. Being direct and clear while communicating with others in a time or situation of conflict can be scary, but there's a smart way to protect your "house," yourself, your friends, to do the right thing when no one else does! I teach girls that *they have the power* to help others by being brave and courageous. Sometimes it's hard for a girl to do the right thing, especially when not everyone else is on board with it. But I always tell girls to stand in their power.

STAND IN YOUR POWER

"Stand in your power!" I say. "Do what feels good to you in your belly, and in most cases your belly doesn't steer you wrong." I talk about responsibility with the girls. Nobody does the right thing all of the time, but we can all try our best. If, for example, you are asked to tell what happened in a certain situation, you can be brave and courageous and report things as you saw them. Or if you've made a mistake it's always best to tell someone about the mistake, even if there are consequences involved. That too, is standing in your power! So I teach the girls about making good choices, like telling the truth or to stand up and take responsibility when they may have made a mistake. I tell them they can always try to do the right thing, even if they have to be brave and courageous or stand alone to do so. As long as they are trying their best to make good decisions, their best is always good enough.

I also talk with the girls and teach them to not worry too much about what others think, especially when it comes to doing the right thing. And at times it's hard to know what to do. I teach the girls that sometimes doing the right thing doesn't make you popular, but that it does mean that you have strong character and can be trusted or will be viewed as someone that is truthful and does the right thing, even when it's difficult. There is inner and outer strength in doing the right thing.

KEEPING SAFE

But I do teach the girls that they should always first and foremost keep themselves safe. Being *smart* is part of Girl Power! As we discussed, if they see someone being picked on but the child that is doing the bullying is bigger or has many friends around them, they can still be brave and courageous by going to get help from an adult. It just means that you may need to work a little harder and be a little more fearless than the rest. I teach girls to love themselves in their weakest and darkest moments and to never ever forget that there is a beautiful light inside of them just dying to get out. They have the ability to let it shine through determination, self-love, kindness and of course by being brave and courageous. I encourage them to let the "warrior" within out because SHE IS AWESOME!

Face-painting "warriors" in the Brave and Courageous class.

IF YOU TEACH THEM, THEY WILL LEARN!

As a result of teaching girls to be brave and courageous, girls have come back and told me stories, like when a new girl arrives at their school:

"Mrs. Mahoney," I was told by a girl, "a new girl started at our school just today. She didn't know anyone so we invited her to sit with us at our lunch table."

Those little acts of kindness help girls to grow and be more accepting.

"I think that's amazing," I told her. ""Why did you do that?"

"Well, we talked about it in your Love and Kindness class, so I just thought it was something that I should do. And I felt great about doing it."

In a conversation like this I always ask the girl how the act of kindness made them feel. "How does it feel when you do the right thing when nobody else does? How does it feel when you do the right thing when no one is looking?"

I love hearing stories from the girls where they do something they've never had to do before and they feel brave. It really makes them feel great. And I tell them, "Sometimes when you make the right decision and no one else does, others will see what you've done and follow. It helps other kids feel confident doing the right thing." I want girls to lead by example. "Other kids get to know that you are a person that they want to be with because they realize you're someone who tells the truth, sticks up for others, and takes responsibility for your own actions. And once you help somebody who needs a little help, they realize you're a person they can go to, you're a person that will have their back." And they will know, "She's the girl that stands in her power and helps others to be brave and courageous too! That's a girl I want to hang out with!"

~

Learning to be brave and courageous is the foundation for not only a girl's power but her ability to show love and kindness, among other things. In fact *all* of the precepts learned in Girl Power work together. And girls that feel frightened, afraid, scared, and maybe even stupid are out there in the world. That's such a horrible feeling, to feel like you're not as smart as the other kids. I know because that was me. Sometimes you just need someone to say that you *are* good enough, you're smart, you're worthy, and you have value. Just because you struggle it doesn't mean you don't have value. It just means you may need to work a little harder and be a little more fearless than the rest.

Class #3: The Power of You

In This Chapter

Class Organization
and Materials

- Part 1: Welcome and Warm Up
- Part 2: Activity
- Part 3: Activity
- Part 4: Fitness
- Part 5: Wrap Up
- Equipment and Materials
- Positive Thoughts

Background
and Theory

- A Girl Power Moment
- What is Power?
- Standing in Power
- The Power of You
- Power Bags
- The Story Behind the Sticky Notes
- Vision Boards
- Power is for Life

CLASS ORGANIZATION AND MATERIALS

PART 1: WELCOME AND WARM UP

Get the Group Moving: Have the group spread out and warm them up. The warm-up should include continuous motion this week. Continuous motion means putting patterns of movement together one after the other to warm up large muscle groups quickly and prepare for plyometric[10] work. All warm up segments in the program help the girls to come together and burn some nervous/excited energy.

Start by having the girls spread out against the wall so they have room to raise their legs in front of them. Instruct them to touch their toes while walking. Have them do light skipping back to the wall. Then have the girls bear-crawl down and inchworm back. In a large room you can have them bear-crawl to the center of the room (gym) and do 10 push-ups then inchworm to the end. Mix it up so that the girls are good and warm for plyometric work. Then call the group to sit in front of you.

––––––––––––––––––––

[10] Plyometrics, also known as "jump training" or "plyos", are exercises in which muscles exert maximum force in short intervals of time, with the goal of increasing power (speed-strength). (https://en.wikipedia.org/wiki/Plyometrics)

<u>Review Homework:</u> If homework was assigned the previous class, go over it together. Encourage the girls to share with the rest of the group.

<u>The Power of You Discussion</u>: What does having your own personal power mean? "Do you realize that even at a young age you have the POWER to influence others? YOU have the power to control aspects of your day." Give the girls examples:

When you wake up in the morning you have a choice. Do you pull the blankets up over your head or do you toss them off and tackle the day? It can go either way but you have the choice, the power! Think about it. If you pull the blankets up will your parents keep coming into your room and telling you to get up for school? Let the girls talk this through. If you stay in bed, what happens? Your parents get angry, you get cranky, and so on. Or do you get yourself out of bed, get ready, eat a healthy breakfast and head out with a great attitude? Mom and Dad are happy, you are happy and you can now rock the day! This is the POWER of YOU in action! Own it! Decide who and where you want to be and GO THERE!

Another scenario to talk through with the girls is how they have the power to decide how to react to others. For example, someone is on their nerves, perhaps a sibling in the morning rush to get off to school. Do they react with harsh words or actions or do they act, meaning take control and remove themselves from the situation? It's a choice—they can simply say, "You are not going to impact my fabulous morning!"

Let the girls share their thoughts and experiences here. Tell the girls to try to use a new method this week whether it is for getting out of bed or interacting with others. They have the POWER to make it an awesome day!

PART 2: ACTIVITY

<u>Things I Love About Me Worksheet:</u> Have the girls spread out and hand out the worksheets. Open the bin of markers and pencils for them to use.

THINGS I LOVE ABOUT ME

I love that I am _____

_____

I love my _____

_____

I love that I am _____

_____

I love my _____

_____

I feel AMAZING when _____

_____

You are AMAZING and SPECIAL

because YOU ARE YOU!

Add in "I Am" Statements Throughout:

- "I am Powerful!"
- "I am Strong!"
- "I am Smart!"
- "I am Special!"
- "I am Unique!"
- and so on—ask for their ideas.

PART 3: ACTIVITY

Power Bags Activity: Each girl gets

- 1 bag
- Sticker sheets for decorating their bag
- 5 or 6 sticky notes (more if they would like and have time)
- Community use of stickers, markers, pencils, and so on.

Ask them to decorate their Power Bags however they want—they can use markers, pencils, stickers, and so on. Be sure to have the girls put their names on the bags somewhere so they can easily find them to take home at the end of class.

Sticky Notes: Each girl gets their sticky notes. Have them write down things they think are amazing about themselves. Then the sticky notes go in the Power Bag. They should be instructed to look at these sticky notes often. This activity is a reminder for them after they leave the class that they have the POWER to be amazing! Also tell them that they should not let anyone tell them different! Be powerful!

Girls should put their "Things I Love About Me" worksheet in their power bags as well.

Insert "I Am" Statements: This is another good time to include a couple more "I Am" statements. Ask for volunteers to come up with words to use.

Clean Up: Have the group help pick up all the supplies and throw away any trash.

Girl Power Girls completing their Power Bags!

PART 4: FITNESS

<u>Encourage:</u> While the girls are doing their plyometrics[11], tell them that the only thing that stands between the start and the finish of ANYTHING is THEM! Decide to succeed and YOU will! Mention the "Think it, Believe it, Achieve it" mantra here. Explain to the girls that they must first get an idea in their minds, *believe* that they can do it, and then find a way to get it done! For example, if someone wants to run a long distance you must first decide to do it. Then you need to convince yourself you can. Put together a training plan to get to the finish line. Then, RUN RIGHT TO IT! Make it happen, achieve it!

<u>Plyometrics:</u> Have the girls line up against the wall. Have them do the following sequences back and forth:

- Skipping down and back. Have them widen the stride here, really stretching the skip, do this three times (expressed in training as "x3").
- Long jumps with arm swings down and back. Try to land lightly.
- High knees down and back.

Then have the girls spread out off the wall and fill the room:

---

[11] **Plyometrics**, also known as "jump training" or "plyos", are exercises in which muscles exert maximum force in short intervals of time, with the goal of increasing power (speed-strength). (https://en.wikipedia.org/wiki/Plyometrics)

- Squat jumps x20: Remind them that their legs will feel very heavy here, but to try and push through, to challenge themselves and know that THEY have the POWER to do it! Have the girls feel their hearts, notice their increased heart rate, and remind them of how strong their bodies are.

- Single leg hops in place x10 on each leg. Ask them, "How does it feel? Is one leg stronger than the other?" Explain how we are not symmetrical and how one side of the body is always stronger than the other. Ask if they can tell which side of them is the strongest. Then explain that their heart is in the middle which means it takes strength from their entire body! Use it wisely!

Include "I Am" Statements: Ask for volunteers to give words

PART 5: WRAP UP

Class Commencement: Have the girls come back together in a group. Give them some positive feedback from the class. Remind them that they have the power to make good decisions, the power to make it a good day, and to remember to read all of the things they wrote and put into their power bags.

Verbally Assign Homework: Practice the POWER of YOU and look forward to sharing what you did to be fabulous next week!

<u>Greet Parents:</u> Greet the parents as they come for pick-up and answer any questions they have. Positive energy and friendliness go a long way!

EQUIPMENT AND MATERIALS

- "Things I Love About Me" worksheet
- Power bags
- Sticky notes
- Stickers
- Marker/pencil bin

POSITIVE THOUGHTS

FOR THE WEEK AND BEYOND!

Know that you have the POWER to inspire others!

Think it, Believe it, Achieve it!

Nothing worth having is achieved without hard work and determination.

BACKGROUND AND THEORY

Fifth-graders, preparing for middle school, create vision boards.

A GIRL POWER MOMENT

ON MY PUBLIC BIO I have been simply including, "veteran." Well at a recent meeting, as we went around the room and introduced ourselves, another woman looked to me and said, "Thanks for serving." It was such a simple thing but so meaningful. My own kids, when they see somebody in uniform they are very respectful—we are very patriotic in our house—and very grateful for those that serve.

But I know that my experience in the military is part of what makes me "Girl Power." I went into a situation where the man to woman ratio was something like 27-to-1. I had things said to me that definitely formed who I was and am today. I worked very hard and went for my staff sergeant stripe early. You had to be nominated by a board to even be eligible, and then you had to do months of study—everything from military history to current affairs. And I did all of the work. Someone very close to me was also competing for a stripe—in fact there were a lot of people going for this stripe on the base at the time. You have to meet all these boards of people and you go through a certain process, but basically they were only giving two stripes away on the base, and it was a big deal—It allows you to promote six months early, and it makes you eligible for your next promotion within your first four years of enlistment which otherwise would not be possible, so it was a big deal. I believe there were about 40 eligible people competing for the two stripes.

It came down to me and a handful of other people, and I ended up getting a stripe. I had worked so hard and literally the last question they asked me—I remember it like it was yesterday—was a current affairs question. I happened to be on the treadmill that morning, and the subject was on the 6 a.m. news. So I knew the story, I had seen it, it was a current affair and it was that day. I answered the question perfectly and with great detail. Later that day I was told I got the stripe. As I shared my excitement, I was then told by a male friend who I trusted and respected, "You got the stripe and this promotion because you were the prettiest one in the shortest skirt." They were wrong, I *earned* that stripe and promotion! There is a huge difference between "getting" and earning.

That was a Girl Power moment. That was a hard one to swallow. It was clear to me at that point that I was in a man's world and no matter how hard I worked, there were those who would always think I was getting what I was getting because I was the "prettiest one in the shortest skirt." And that was just *so* not the case. I *earned* that stripe. When he said that to me, I was very young but I stood in my power and I said, "You are so mistaken. I earned that stripe because I worked and paid attention for all these months, and I knew my stuff. And that's why I got it."

I earned that stripe and promotion because I was the most qualified candidate. I worked the hardest, studied the most, and kept going, researching, learning, and listening until the very end of the process! The key is to not allow or let people kill your dreams or take your power with their words or actions. We can only control our own words and actions and standing in your power often means blocking out the noise and negativity of others. There are always going to be naysayers, and "haters." It's not always easy, but you must try to let those people go. Let them fade away when they are not being loving and kind. Focus on those that make you feel supported and your best. Clearly, that experience was a defining moment for me and has been part of who I have become. I had a choice to either believe what I was told and feel disappointed and hurt, or to stand in my power and light, and remember that I did not and am not "getting" things because I look best in the shortest skirt, but because I work really hard! I just happen to also look really great in a skirt—bonus!

WHAT IS POWER?

So what is power, anyway? What is power for an eight to thirteen-year-old girl, or for anyone for that matter? I think power is doing what feels best to you in the moment and then learning from things, learning from success as well as from mistakes and failure. The Girl Power program is called Girl Power partly because it was born from a place of needing to show a little girl her very real, very big power! Power is the energy that we create in the thoughts that we keep in our head. Positive thought brings positive action! Maybe you look at something and you might have done it differently the next time, but I always teach girls that it's okay to make mistakes. And if we've made a mistake and feel someone needs to know about it we must be brave and tell them. We need to let them know despite the fear. If we take responsibility and acknowledge our own mistakes, that's huge, that's power! Power is being true to yourself and doing the best that you can in any given moment. And your best is always good enough! It's loving yourself at every stage and knowing that you are exactly where you should be in this moment.

Power is being able to stand in your place or light, wherever that is at any given moment where you feel most comfortable and confident, and to really not care about what others think. That's a hard thing to learn because kids want to fit in and be accepted.. I tell girls it's okay to not care about what everybody else thinks. It doesn't mean you're not caring or loving or sensitive, it means you are standing in your space and you are deciding first what is meaningful and true to *you*, and then moving from there. "This is my power, this is where I want to be, where I choose to be."

Power is also knowing that we are all going to make mistakes and we're all flawed, and we can't possibly do everything right, yet teaching girls to really love themselves at every stage. I have that as one of the positive thoughts for the girls to take with them, whether it's "Love your body," or "Love yourself," love YOU at every stage because you and your body are always changing.

So many girls would never dream of loving their flaws. Immediately our minds go to beating ourselves up. "Oh, how could I have done that? Why would I do such a stupid thing? I can't do anything right! I stink!" But I want girls to know that if you don't make mistakes you don't grow or learn. Every mistake is an opportunity to grow, to do better, to show up in your beautiful light, in that power that you are meant to have and feel! This is the POWER of YOU in action! Own it! Decide who and where you want to be and GO THERE, embracing the flaws and mistakes, taking responsibility for all of your actions and loving the ride!

STANDING IN POWER

Sometimes I don't think we let our kids stand in their power. I've had this happen with my kids, wondered if I should kind of make my son sleep over someplace when he didn't want to. He explained to me, "Mom, it's okay. I don't want to sleep over—I don't care what those other kids say." And there's something very empowering about that! I'm so proud of him that he knows what he does and doesn't want to do and he makes that the most important factor in his decision making. I think sometimes, when a kid chooses to go against what all the other kids are doing because they just don't feel comfortable, that's them, standing in their power. You know, showing up and saying, "This is what I want to do. So it's great that everyone else loves a sleepover, I just don't and want to go home," and then feeling happy and confident with and about their decision. It's brave, it's independent, it's confident. It's a way for a child to stand in their power!

Another example of a child standing in their power might be if they don't want to do things that other kids are doing, like hanging around at the local library after school or going out to lunch with a big group of kids on half days. It's not only okay it's important for kids to do what *they* want to do based on their desires versus doing what they think other kids or their parents want them to do. But sometimes parents worry if a child decides not to attend a dance or activity or go to the library or out for lunch on a half day with the crowd. You might worry, "Will they have regrets? What if everyone else is doing it? What will the other kids think?" Well this is me and Girl Power saying, "Who cares what the other kids think! Who cares what other parents think for that matter!" If a girl or any child says, "This is what I really want to do," then I would let them do it their way. It gives them an opportunity to show up the way they want to. It's an opportunity to be powerful and stand in their light on their terms. Keep the lines of communication wide open but let them makes some of these decisions on their own too.

THE POWER OF YOU

Class 3, "The Power of You," or the "Power Class" is one of the girls' favorite classes and one where girls seem to continue to use the lessons they learn in Girl Power for years and years to come, hopefully throughout their entire lives. I've had parents as well as girls who have taken this program tell me that they still revert back the activity and lessons they learned in the "Power of You" class. The "The Power of You" is a lesson plan where we talk about how even at a young age kids have the power to change the direction of their day as soon as they wake up. YOU, we demonstrate, have the power to make it an awesome day, whether it be with their friends or just by themselves, and in whatever they choose to do.

Before we do our activities, I talk to the girls and ask them, "What do you think that means when I say, The Power of You? Do you think that you are powerful?" And if I'm talking to girls who are nine, ten, or eleven years-old, I let them know that I understand that they are at a very young age, sometimes they might feel like they have no power. I give them examples of how they have power and might say something like, "Let's talk about getting ready for school. You know, you *have* to go to school because mom and dad say you do, that's kind of your job." But I help them realize that even at a young age kids have the power to set the tone for the day. "Will it be a good day or a bad day? It's largely based on how you decide to behave. If you pull the blankets up over your head and say you aren't getting out of bed how do you think the day is going to go? You have the power to get out of the house on time, to make it a very calm morning." I'll ask them, "If it's cold or rainy and your bed is super cozy, can you stay in bed if you want to? I know that you want to pull those blankets up over your head and say, 'Ugh! I'm not going to school today, I don't want to get up!' But what do you think will happen if you do that? Will Mom and Dad be happy? Will tempers flare and will there be shouting? Maybe even tears?"

So I talk them through: "So tell me what happens. Finish this sentence: 'If I stay in bed, Mom is going to get _____.'" This becomes a lot of fun as they give me answers. We talk about what the outcomes might be if they choose to stay in bed and fuss or, if they jump up and hustle. In the end they must go to school so best to do it in a way that is positive and enjoyable for everyone! This discussion gives girls a clear picture of how they can use their power in positive ways every day, how they can make a good decision even if it's as simple as pulling the covers off and getting ready for school versus staying in bed and causing unhappiness. It's THE POWER OF YOU!

POWER BAGS

For this class, I created an exercise to help girls get into a positive, self-loving frame of mind. The girls each have a worksheet that begins with "The Things I Love About Me." They fill in the blanks in the incomplete sentences I have provided. Then, using a small paper gift bag with handles and sticky notes (Post-Its), the girls create a "Power Bag." They put positive affirmations on sticky notes and put the sticky notes in and on the bag for later. I stamp different words on the bags like "Imagine," "Strength," and "You Rock!" and I tell them, "You rock! You have the power to rock every day. Don't just go *through* your day, *rock* the day!"

So they put all these sticky notes in there and I tell them to take them out and put them on their mirror at home. I have heard from parents and girls years after they leave the Girl Power Program that they keep these sticky notes on their mirrors, headboards, walls and so on. I have received countless pictures and emails of girls' sticky notes and it never gets old for me. Knowing that this powerful exercise continues to inspire, encourage, and support girls that have participated in the Girl Power program brings tears of joy to my eyes every time!

I have a mom who sent me a picture a month or two after her daughter had done my class. One evening I was home, it was about 10:30 at night and I got a text on my phone from a mom and it said, "I just have to let you know the impact that you're having on girls." And it was a picture of her daughter's bedroom. This mom found when she went to tuck her daughter in to bed, that her daughter had been writing sticky notes and they were stuck all over her headboard. They read, "I am strong. I am powerful. I am beautiful," and even more along those lines. Recently I had twins in my classroom and their mother sent me a similar note. She also sent pictures of the girls' bedroom. They too had sticky notes all over their wall, above their beds. She shared that they read them every day before school. They said things like, "I'm brave, I'm silly, I'm beautiful, I'm strong, I'm a good helper," and "I'm a good sister."

It's so important to instill in our children that they are powerful, valuable beings. Giving them the tools they need to create a positive, daily practice is the work that I love. You are what you think, so think positive, loving thoughts! When And to this day as I receive notes, emails, texts and pictures from parents I think, *Awesome. Just awesome!*

THE STORY BEHIND THE STICKY NOTES

I always use an analogy to help the girls understand why we are doing a lesson or having a discussion. For the sticky notes exercise, I always sit down on the floor with them and I tell them this little story. The Power Bag and sticky notes activity started when I went into the military when I was younger, and I became very homesick. So I tell the girls the following story:

> "You know, when I was seventeen years old, my mom actually had to sign for me and give me permission to enter the United States Air Force because I was not eighteen yet, I was a minor. What I didn't think about or realize was that while I wanted to serve my country and I could get my education through the military, they might ship me off to some far-away place, and they did! They sent me to a place where I didn't know anybody. So at seventeen that was really scary.
>
> "But I couldn't just come home, as if I was in college and homesick, you know. I was in the military. So I began to write things on sticky notes and put them all over my dormitory and later in my apartment, just to kind of make me feel less lonely, but also and probably more importantly to make me feel good. One of the things my mom used to say to me as she sent me off to the school bus was 'Make it a fantastic day!' or she might

73

wake me up and say 'You have a beautiful smile' or if I was having a tough time she would say something like 'You are amazing. You are a great daughter,' or You are a great sister.'

"I remember specifically I put in my bathroom, 'You have a beautiful smile,' and 'Make it an amazing day!' Those were some of my most powerful and favorite sticky notes because they reminded me of less lonely times and made me feel less homesick. Those little notes made me feel somehow closer to family—my mother in particular—and helped me enjoy my days. Every day I would forget that the notes were there, but I would go into the bathroom in the morning to get cleaned up or brush my teeth, and when you see a sign you read it! It would immediately bring a smile to my face. It would make me feel there was a piece of home there with me, and I wasn't so alone. What I didn't realize at the time was that it was affirming so many positive things about me on the inside whenever I was doing the daily practice of positive thinking."

VISION BOARDS

Vision boards are the next step. I ask girls to collect things that they love—"What are your favorite sports? What words make you feel strong and powerful? Do you have people in your life that make you feel strong, powerful, supported and loved?" And then, taking all of those things—I bring some materials and they bring some materials—we take a poster board and we decorate it with markers or a bunch of things they can cut and paste, tape, or whatever they want to do. I then tell them to display their boards somewhere, where they will see them often.

POWER IS FOR LIFE

Teaching girls this foundation to be powerful at a young age will help them all throughout their lives. Even myself, as a wife, as a mother, as a woman—young girls grow into older girls who grow into women—I think part of why I do what I do is because of the road that I've traveled. I saw my mom busting her hump, and at times she didn't have confidence, but somehow she gave my sister and I self-confidence. It's important to know that it's okay to take care of yourself in whatever way serves you. For example, if going to the gym makes you feel like a rock star or superhero for the rest of the day then make it a priority! Figure out whatever it is that makes you feel your best and DO IT! By doing so we are going to be better equipped to take care of everyone else that needs us. By teaching these life lessons to girls earlier in life they will be better to themselves, especially as they take on more responsibility. We are laying the groundwork and creating communities of strong girls who will grow into strong women!

.

CLASS #4: GOOD FRIENDS AND NAVIGATING RELATIONSHIPS

IN THIS CHAPTER

CLASS ORGANIZATION

AND MATERIALS

- Part 1: Welcome and Warm Up
- Part 2: Activity
- Part 3: Activity
- Part 3: Fitness
- Part 4: Team-Oriented Fitness Games
- Part 5: Wrap Up
- Equipment and Materials
- Worksheet and Exercise
- Positive Thoughts

BACKGROUND

AND THEORY

- Choose to Be a Good Friend
- Paying it Forward
- Room for Change
- Open Hearts, Open Minds
- The Problem of Three
- Crumpled
- Better Friends for Life

CLASS ORGANIZATION AND MATERIALS

PART 1: WELCOME AND WARM UP

<u>Get the Group Moving:</u> Have the group spread out and warm them up with dynamic stretching, jumping jacks, running in place or laps around the room, then static stretching. Do these for 3-5 minutes to warm them up and help them burn some nervous/excited energy.

<u>Hula Hoop and Tennis Ball</u>: Then split the group up into pairs of two. Give each group a hula hoop and a tennis ball. Have both girls stand inside the hula hoop with the hula hoop around their waists. Have one bounce the ball within the hula hoop while the other catches it. The objective is to have them work together to keep the ball within their control. If the ball gets away, they have to move and work together to go get the ball and resume the game. They must both remain in the hula hoop at all times. This teaches teamwork and problem solving while working together. Have the girls do this for 5-10 minutes then have them sit in front of you as a group.

<u>Review Homework:</u> If homework was assigned the previous class, go over it together. Encourage the girls to share with the rest of the group.

<u>Overview:</u> Once the girls come together give an overview of what this class is all about. The girls will be given tools to make good friends while being one. They will learn about the

power of leading by example. Discuss navigating relationships in a way that is caring and thoughtful while being good to yourself and others.

PART 2: ACTIVITY

Index Card Activity: Have the girls sit in a large circle. Each girl gets one index card and a marker or colored pencil. The girls should write down the quality that they feel is most important in a friend. Prompt some examples such as:

- Trustworthy,
- Honest,
- Funny,
- Loyal,
- Kind.

Have them fold the card until everyone is done and it is time to share. Once they have all written something down begin to encourage them to share what they wrote. The instructor should share what she feels is a good quality in a friend here. A good way to get the girls discussing different qualities and why they feel they are important in a friend is to ask them to raise their hands to questions like, "Who wrote down honest as a quality?" for example. From there, continue to see what the similarities are and ask the girls to share what they wrote. It's amazing to see what others view as important qualities in a friend and to discuss why.

How to Be a Good Friend Sheet: Then hand out and review the "How to be a Good Friend" printout. This always prompts lots of discussion and sharing from the girls. Review the hand out and let the girls share examples of when they had someone be a good friend, when *they* themselves might have been a good friend, or when someone was not a good friend. This is another great time to let them explore their own relationships and feelings. Give them tips on how to improve communication and interaction with others.

Paper Crush Activity: After the review and discussion of the "How to be a Good Friend" sheet do the paper crush activity. Make it fun and surprise the girls. Have them take the "How to be a Good Friend" sheet and crinkle it up in their hands. Tell them not to rip it but to crush it. Then they should drop it on the floor and step on it. Mush it into the floor and try to flatten it under their shoe. Then have them pick it up and put it into their open palm. Look at it and tell them "This paper is your very best friend!"

Have them say sorry to it. Seems silly but they will say things like, "I would never treat my friend like that." After crushing and stomping on the paper, instruct the girls to try to clean the paper and flatten in out—basically, to fix it or get it back the way that it was originally.

This is a visual lesson that you will talk through with the girls. It demonstrates that once you do something, or say something, no matter how hard you might try to fix it you can't get it back to the way that it was. It will be impossible for them to get the paper completely flat or clean and this is a great demonstration of how our actions speak louder than words in a sense. Discuss "think before you speak" here and how it is important to be thoughtful and kind with both words and actions.

Let them share here. They often have a lot to say. The group really comes together here as many of the girls realize that they are dealing with the same issues in many social circles. Finish this discussion by talking with the girls about "strength in numbers." Help them to understand that when they come together and make good decisions others will follow. Peer pressure at every age is difficult but given the tools to stand up for what is right is easier when you feel supported by the people around you.

PART 3: ACTIVITY

Good Qualities Cards: Each girl gets the following materials:

- 1 printout of the Good Qualities list
- 1 piece of card stock
- Scissors
- Glue stick
- Community use of markers, pencils, etc.

Ask them to cut out each bubble and decorate their cards however they want. They can use markers, pencils, fun cut scissors, and so on.

Or (alternate exercise), BFF Picture Frames: Each girl gets the following materials:

- 1 BFF picture frame
- 1 printout of the Good Qualities list
- Foam stickers (baggies)
- Glitter markers
- Community use of stickers, markers, pencils, and so on.

Ask them to decorate their picture frames however they want. They can use markers, pencils, stickers.

Insert "I Am" Statements: This is a good time to include "I Am" statements. Ask for volunteers to come up with words to use. Examples would be kind, trustworthy, loyal, proud, smart, or strong.

Clean Up: Have the group help pick up all the supplies and throw away any trash.

PART 4: TEAM-ORIENTED FITNESS GAMES

Tennis Ball Running Game: Have the girls break into groups and set tennis balls on low profile cones. The game is progressive so begin with only one cone and one tennis ball placed in the center of the room. The girls will count off and be broken into teams, then place half of the team on one end of the room and half on the other end. The cone with the ball is in the middle.

The game begins with one girl running to the cone, picking up the ball and passing to her teammate on the other end. That girl takes the ball, runs to the cone and replaces the ball then runs to her teammate on the opposite end of the room. They high five and that girl runs to the cone, picks up the ball and so on and so forth until all the girls have completed a run with pick up and placement. When they are done they should sit.

Then add another cone and ball. Re-space them so they are evenly spread out within the given space. Run through the game again. Then add a third ball. It's hard for the girls to run, place, and pick up three tennis balls so the team is encouraged to cheer them on and give tips. There are no prizes just the benefits of working together and feeling a part of something to reach a common goal!

Or (alternate exercise), Two or Three Girl Tennis Ball Toss: Have the girls break into groups of two or pair them up. Each team of two gets a tennis ball. They should begin by playing catch but close together. Talk to them about reading their partner and working together to make both good catches and throws. Then have each girl take three steps back. Now they should try to continue the catch game and add one bounce in-between them. They will need to toss it just right to get it to their partner without it going too far or falling short. Either way the girls should have fun. They should continue to move further apart every two to three minutes. If you have an uneven number, do teams of three.

Include "I Am" Statements: Ask for volunteers to give words. Examples would be, honest, a good friend, thoughtful, beautiful.

PART 5: WRAP UP

Class Commencement: Have the girls come back together in a group. Give them some positive feedback from the class. Remind them that they have the power to be a good friend as well as make them. Remind them to do the right thing even when no one else does. Encourage them to make good decisions and always try to think before they speak.

Verbally Assign Homework: "Be good to yourself and others. Think before you speak and be fabulous! Remember that you are strong but there is also strength in numbers! Try to do something this week that makes you a great friend!"

Greet Parents: Greet the parents as they come for pick-up and answer any questions they have. Positive energy and friendliness go a long way!

EQUIPMENT AND MATERIALS

- Index cards (if this activity has been chosen)
- Good Quality printout and card stock **OR** BFF picture frames (based on which activity is chosen)
- "How to be a Good Friend" printout
- Marker/pencil bin
- Glue sticks
- Foam stickers
- Scissors
- Hula hoops
- Tennis balls
- Low profile cones

Worksheet and Exercise

This is a transformational class for girls, Good Friends and Navigating Relationships. We begin the class with an activity and I have a "How to Be a Good Friend" sheet. I put things on there that I myself really look for in good friends and I think they've been very relatable to the girls. There are eleven points and we take our time to talk about each one. We go around the room and have the girls each read one, and we talk about them as we go. At the top it says, "To have good friends, you must be a good friend. Here are some ways good friends treat each other," and then it goes on with those eleven things:

> To have good friends you must <u>be</u> a good friend.
>
> Here are some ways good friends treat each other:

1. *Good friends listen to each other.*
2. *Good friends don't put each other down or hurt each other's feelings.*
3. *Good friends try to understand each other's feelings and moods.*
4. *Good friends help each other solve problems.*
5. *Good friends give each other compliments.*
6. *Good friends can disagree without hurting each other.*
7. *Good friends are dependable.*
8. *Good friends respect each other.*
9. *Good friends are trustworthy.*
10. *Good friends give each other room to change.*
11. *Good friends care about each other.*

POSITIVE THOUGHTS

FOR THE WEEK AND BEYOND!

Be true to yourself and others.

All things that bring us great joy require hard work.

Good friends stand by you in all situations.

BACKGROUND AND THEORY

CHOOSE TO BE A GOOD FRIEND

CLASS #4, GOOD FRIENDS and Navigating Relationships, is one of my favorite classes (But I think I say that about every class, because I love them all!). This class really is one of the most valuable classes that I teach. A lot of the feedback is such that the girls can take the lesson and go and apply it right away. It's an important class at any age, because what girl hasn't struggled with other girls? It's tough—relationships are tough at any age, and we all know at times girls of all ages can be mean to each other, even grown women! So I try to teach this class from a place of love and care. I try to teach from the place of "How can you be a good friend, and what does being a good friend mean to you?" I then help them to apply that idea and to also realize that they have this incredible choice, to choose who their friends are. Not to say that they would be mean to someone or not be friends with them, but that they can stand tall and say, "This is what friendship means to me. This is how I treat my friends and I expect others to treat me in that same way."

I think a lot of kids—girls and boys—don't realize that they have the right and the power to choose who they are friends with. Just because someone is in your classes or at your bus stop doesn't mean that they are a great fit for you and you *must* be friends with them. I teach kids to always be kind and caring but choose your tribe. Decide who you are most aligned with and choose to develop strong friendships with those kids. Friendship isn't automatic, it's something that grows from common interests and values, kindness, behavior and communication. I teach kids that it's okay to hold our friends to certain expectations or values, but also to always start with themselves, from within. And if our girls are behaving that way, they are going to attract like-minded people and create amazing friendships!

PAYING IT FORWARD

And the place where Girl Power really got its start was with like-minded people, with the Girl Scouts. It's such a great fit, after all. Some girls move away from it as they go through middle school—they get involved in other things, they do clubs at school and so on—but you can see that the girls who stick with it are taught about leadership as they become adults, about taking responsibility not only for themselves but for others. They practice all of these principles that I try to teach girls, about being kind, about taking the best care of yourself, how it feels to be strong and healthy.

In the Love and Kindness class I talk about paying it forward, even if it's as simple as paying for someone's coffee that's behind you in the drive-thru. It can be as simple as holding a door open for somebody. And something I do in the Love and Kindness class is I have them make cards for no reason. It can't be a birthday card or an anniversary card—it has to be something else. Maybe it's just a "thank you" because Mom or Dad makes you breakfast every day or because you have clean clothes, because they are taking really good care of you. There are a lot of kids that don't have basic things, and teaching the girls to appreciate and be grateful is important. It's also about teaching them to say it out loud and express it, because it can make someone feel so valued. You have the opportunity to make someone's day by making them feel special.

I also want girls to experience how it makes *them* feel to surprise someone with kindness or to do something kind and not tell anyone—how good that feels on the inside. I love when they come back to class and share the ways they did this for the week but most importantly I love how they express it, sometimes so animated and always sincere and with great joy. I don't even have to ask them how it felt to do it because I can see it and I know they feel it! So that's one important principle to instill in this particular class.

When they come back the next day I love to hear all the stories the girls come up with. Some want to act on this right away. For example, some want to thank their teachers and are so excited they want to go put a thank you card on their teacher's desk. I have to tell them, "You can't run around your school. Put it in your backpack, you won't forget. Give it to them tomorrow." But when they leave class they are very excited and they can't wait to get back after practicing kind actions and talk about how good it makes them feel, and that's the surprise for them, they don't expect that piece. But once they do it, once they make that kind gesture, one that is unexpected and they tell nobody else, that feeling becomes natural. It becomes part of them. I see the transformation over and over, how a girl who might have been less open to doing something for someone else now wants to go out of her way to make someone feel special or cared for. I tell them

"Don't forget that feeling, and do it often. Remind people that you care about them and why."

I, for example, have great memories of my mother. And while I'm sad that she's not here, the memories are the things she instilled in me. She said such positive things to us at bedtime, when she tucked us in. I recall the things that she didn't have to do but she did, because I know they made her feel good. I teach kids this is your way of showing people you care about them. Words are the easy part. It's our actions that make us feel good inside, that make us really decide who we want to be and how we want to impact others. Again, teaching them this at a very young age is important. Even the youngest girls I work with make cards that are heartfelt and raw, and those are such treasures to the person that they shared them with. They are treasures to me!

ROOM FOR CHANGE

Another important principle is "Friends give each other room to change." And a funny thing often happens when I teach this class to younger girls. Children are so literal. When it says, "Friends give each other room to change." We always talk about it in depth with the younger girls, as they don't usually get it. This is how it sometimes plays out. A girl might ask or say, "Does that mean change our clothes? She goes in her room to change, like, my friend is coming over to swim and she has to change?" You know, in first and second grade, that's what they think about! So we talk it over, and it's really kind of sweet and funny. It always reminds me of their innocence and how much they still have to learn. It's so fantastic to have an opportunity to share these lessons with them for perhaps the first time or at least when it's somewhat new to them.

When I share this with the older girls who understand the meaning of the phrase they always get a giggle out of it. That often helps to create a relaxed atmosphere for the girls where they are more open to share their personal experiences. Girl relationships can be difficult, but when you find friends that are worth it you put forth the effort—always worth it! One of the most important things I teach the girls throughout this entire program is to stay true to themselves and then I arm them with the tools to do that.

I try to explain to them "If you have a friend and you've been friends for a long time, you both might change over time. Maybe you were friends in preschool and kindergarten, but then maybe in the fourth grade you might not have so many things in common. Maybe one of you loves sports and the other loves an instrument, or as you get older, maybe one of you goes for student council and one of you wants to be in the chess club and learn Spanish. It's okay, but not always easy to let friends change." It doesn't mean they're not friends anymore.

I think it takes a really good friend to let things change. I teach the girls that it's important to let each other grow into the person they are supposed to be and still find a way to maintain and nourish your friendship. It's important to find new ways to be together and enjoy each other's company as each girl changes and grows. Open hearts and open minds!

OPEN HEARTS, OPEN MINDS

All things that bring us great joy require hard work. So I talk to them about that because sometimes relationships require hard work. Just because a relationship doesn't flow easily doesn't mean it's not a relationship worth keeping or worth working at. Being able to communicate as we navigate through relationships is important in teaching girls how to navigate through things, especially difficult things. Maybe they don't get along or they see things differently. Maybe they encounter a mean girl or have a mean girl episode. It's important to know how to get through that and know the difference between putting your best effort forward because this is a person we actually do want to have a friendship or a relationship with, and knowing when to say, "This is too much, this isn't a relationship that is going to be valuable to me." *Good* friends stand by each other in all situations. Good friends do not have to always agree but they should always be respectful of each other and their differences.

We talk about examples, we talk through things, like if there's a new student in school, and maybe they see them in the lunchroom or on the bus. These can be very tricky places because a lot of things go down in those places! And by "go down," I mean that kids can say and do things in those busy places at school or on the bus and get away with more. Even with appropriate supervision things can be said by kids that they would not dream of saying face-to-face with an adult. Hurtful or mean things often happen in those places. These are two of my least favorite places in school for kids because things happen there that wouldn't ordinarily happen in other places. However, the cafeteria and bus are also great places for girls to meet a challenge, to be brave, to do the right thing and to be a good friend. They are also great places to invite someone else to be a good friend or do the right thing

THE PROBLEM OF THREE

We talk about the "Problem of Three," which is kind of an offshoot class form the Friendship class. It's about helping children to navigate when conflicts arise in groups of three. Sometimes it's the girl who gets left out that feels bad or hurt. Other times it's the girl who everyone is fighting for the attention of that gets hurt. Both can be tough spots to be in. People don't think of that, they just automatically think that with three someone gets left out and hurt, which very often is the case, but when two girls want the attention of one girl, that can be a sticky situation too. Either way the one in the middle is trying to find the balance. So we talk about that, about being open to learning about new people, about the "Problem of Three" and strategic ways to navigate through that with girls, about how to be kind to everyone involved while still standing in your power!

A lot of girls share stories about dealing with those issues and I tell them, "If you have a friend that you like and you care about, and she likes this other friend, you should give that other friend a chance. Let them in because that just might be an opportunity for you to make and have another really good friend. You value what this other person thinks, right? You like this person, and she probably makes really good decisions. So maybe this other girl is a great girl too. You will never know if you shut down and get in your own way. Be open to discovering new relationships. It's an opportunity to widen your circle." I am always teaching them to have an open heart and an open mind.

I always tell them that you never know where your next best friend is going to be—they could be sitting right next to you and you might not even know it! This girl in the sixth grade that you've just met could be your bestie in the years ahead in middle school, but if you're not open to that, you might not discover it, you might miss it. I try to get them excited about that. I help them turn insecurity, fear, and nervousness into excitement. I get lots of hands going up when I ask, "Has anyone here ever had a disagreement with a friend?" And just like that, they're all just waiting to spill it! "I was on the playground and Lily wasn't nice to me!" And we explain and reinforce what they *can* do with a powerful exercise.

CRUMPLED

I teach girls to think before they speak. I tell them, "Here is something to think about: Once you say something and the words leave your lips you can't take them back. Think before you speak." I am always throwing that in, in this class (Class #4, Good Friends and Navigating Relationships) and the next (Class #5, Love and Kindness). So we do the index card activity, we discuss the "How to be a Good Friend" printout, and what we do next with this sheet of paper is a visual lesson that's fun for the girls. We have the physical paper and we go over all of these various important statements and tips on how to be a good friend and how to choose a good friend and we talk about each one of them. We talk about how I

think it's very important that we think before we speak,
because that's really difficult, and we talk about what that
really means. We talk about how once something comes out
of your mouth—even if after saying it you feel bad about it
and you then try to talk through it with a friend—the
relationship is still different. Once it comes out of your
mouth you can't take it back. It's out there! You and your
friend can talk and move past it by practicing forgiveness but
the friendship may not feel exactly the same with that friend,
at least for a bit. Over time hopefully it does, but I stress how
important it is for the girls to "think before you speak!"

So we take the "How to be a Good Friend" printout (and
it's funny how quickly they attach to it!) and I then have them
crumple it up. I have them put it on the floor and kind of
stomp on it. The girls do this and they get the paper
crumpled and a little bit dirty, and I then have them hold it in
the palm of their hand and I say, "Imagine that this paper is
your very best friend." Now keep in mind that some girls
don't want to crumple the paper in the first place, never mind
stomp on it or get it dirty. They "like" the paper and don't
want to ruin it.

When I ask them to pretend this is their very best friend
you can hear the gasps. They all kind of inhale, "My gosh! I
would never treat my friend like that!" And then their task is
to unfold the paper very carefully trying not to rip it. By now
they've pressed it into a tiny ball, but they now want to undo
it, trying to unfold it carefully. They try to flatten it out, and
we talk about how it's a little bit dirty, a little different, and
how no matter what they do, they cannot get it back to
exactly the way it was before they stomped on it and they
crumpled it up. We talk about how that's the same thing as

your relationship—you're trying to fix it, you're trying to clean it off, you're trying, but it's still a little bit different. And that's why it's really, really, important to think before you speak, because your words have power and they impact others. You want to use them in a way that's kind and caring, even in moments of anger or disagreement.

Now really, for kids, that is like, "Oh, my gosh!" and some of the girls want to take a sheet home but they don't want to take the one they ruined. "Well, I could take it home and iron it," they say. And they really get the point, it's impactful.

BETTER FRIENDS FOR LIFE

So these are two really fun classes (Class #4 and Class #5) to teach but also classes that I feel have great impact. I'm hoping that they help girls to see how powerful they are, that it empowers them. I hope that it gives them that feeling that you really can't teach, that light heart to just know you have made a difference in another human being's life. It's about what you feel like when you are really loving and kind, and have an open heart. These are the moments they take with them well beyond my classroom as they have learned the "good lessons" and they will have them forever! It's the point of impact, the point of change for the better, the *power* of Love and Kindness!

My wish, my hope, is always that they want to feel those things more often. It feels much better to be a good friend or to be someone who approaches things from a calm, caring place, whatever the situation might be. It's really powerful to be the one that people look to and say, "Wow, that's a girl who takes the high road, who does the right thing, who knows why she acted in a kind way. She also stood up for herself and she stands up for her friends too." Girls want to be friends with girls who stick up for themselves and stick up for others. I teach girls to be friends with a girl who will have your back. As well as being that girl yourself!

It's the same with adults. We want to surround ourselves with people who are like-minded but also people who care enough to kind of go out on the skinny branch, to go to that place where maybe it doesn't make you popular but they go there anyway. Why? Because they care enough to not worry about what other people think. They do what feels right in their gut. Those are the things that are hard to teach, so I do it in many ways: in the activities that we do, the lesson plans; and even in the physical activities that let them get out energy and enforce the life lessons in the class.

The kids love this class, it's powerful for them, and it helps them move ahead with those thoughts in their heads, that they have the power to make other kids feel really good, and that makes *you* feel good. but it starts with "How can I be a good friend? How can I take responsibility for my actions?" There are so many scenarios out there, where girls are looking for ways to figure these things out. The skills that they are learning in the Good Friends and Navigating Relationships class will help them and serve them for the rest of their lives.

One of my favorite positive thoughts is "Strong Body, Strong Mind, Strong You." It's about taking care of that whole person. Another is "Being kind to others shows how strong you are inside and out." I think that's something that makes Girl Power special. We give the girls the tools and activities to practice these life lessons and skills. The activities show them the power of how it feels to be good to somebody else for any reason, big or small, and how far that goes. And I tell them, "Do one kind thing every day for someone else. Being kind to others makes you feel great about yourself. It fills your heart with love in such a way that you feel it throughout your whole body! The kindest gift in life is love. Love yourself, love your family, and love your friends."

You hear all of these things, the "Law of Attraction," and what makes people feel worthy and special, and it's all the same thing, and it should be taught to them while they are young. I believe in the good old fashioned, "Do unto others as you would have done unto you." It's an amazing way to approach the relationships in your life.

CLASS #5: LOVE AND KINDNESS

IN THIS CHAPTER

CLASS ORGANIZATION

AND MATERIALS

- Part 1: Welcome and Warm Up
- Part 2: Discussion
- Part 3: Activity
- Part 4: Fitness
- Part 5: Wrap Up
- Equipment and Materials
- Positive Thoughts

BACKGROUND

AND THEORY

- More Bees with Honey
- Mean Girls
- The Mean Girl
- My Own Love and Kindness Breakthrough
- Checking In

CLASS ORGANIZATION AND MATERIALS

PART 1: WELCOME AND WARM UP

Get the Group Moving: Have the group spread out and warm up with dynamic stretching, jumping jacks, running in place or laps around the room, then static stretching. Do this for 3-5 minutes to warm them up and help them burn some nervous/excited energy.

Review Homework: If homework was assigned the previous class, go over it together. Encourage the girls to share with the rest of the group.

PART 2: DISCUSSION

Love and Kindness Discussion: Following the warm up, begin this class with the girls sitting in a circle. Have them come together and explain the theme of the class. It's important to let the girls relax and be open to sharing their experiences for this class. Ask them to share things that they have done that come from the heart. Have them give examples of when they have been kind and loving recently. Also give examples to get them started. Let the discussion flow here as you pass out the supplies for the activity.

Random Acts of Kindness Discussion: Explain "paying it forward" and what that means—to do something for no other reason than because it feels good in your heart or right in your mind. For example, ask the girls if they have ever seen their parents pay for a person's coffee in the drive-thru. If not, explain that Erin, the creator of Girl Power does that sometimes. She surprises the person behind her by asking what they ordered and paying for it just because it's a nice thing to do. She only does it once in a while but it's fun and feels good. Imagine how surprised and excited you might be if someone did that for you or your parents. Wouldn't that be nice? It's like spreading good karma to strangers. Maybe they will be inspired to do something nice for someone that day or sometime soon.

Be nice to someone in your classroom that might be shy or quiet. Extend yourself and see how it makes others feel happy and accepted. Invite someone new to sit with you at the lunch table or encourage your friends to be kind to kids outside of your current friend circle. Be open to meeting others and accepting each other's differences.

Be kind and loving to your parents and siblings. This can be one that brings on some fun discussions. Let the girls tell their stories and see how they have similarities to each other. This helps the girls to realize that they are not alone and that others struggle with the same things at home and with friends as well. You want to teach them that "It's all in how you look at it." Explain to the girls that if they step back in a difficult situation and really try to view it in a loving and kind way it's never as bad or as big as they initially thought. It takes practice but is worth the effort! Feel free to add your own experiences to relate to your class as well.

Discuss all of these situations with the girls and help them to understand the power of love and kindness and how it can help them to feel strong and confident inside.

PART 3: ACTIVITY

Card Activity for "No Reason": Each girl gets the following materials:

- Scrapbook pages or card stock
- Stickers
- Community use of markers/pencils
- Scissors
- Glue Sticks

The girls make a 'love and kindness' card in this class for someone in their life that they care about. This activity helps the girls to understand the concepts above. Doing something kind and loving for someone for no reason is good for the soul and feels good in your heart! Discuss people in their lives that support them every day but that they might not thank in this way—Mom and Dad, a sibling, a teacher, a friend or a coach, for example.

Ask the girls, "Who made your breakfast this morning?" or "Who helped you with homework last night? Wouldn't it be nice to say thank you? Wouldn't they be surprised to get a thank you from you? How do you think that would make them feel? Wouldn't they feel great to get an 'I love you' or 'I appreciate you' card?"

Insert "I Am" Statements: While they are making their card is a good time to include "I Am" statements. Ask for volunteers to come up with words to use, such as "kind, loving, caring," and so on.

Clean Up: Have the group help pick up all the supplies and throw away any trash.

PART 4: FITNESS

Core Work, Boot Camp Work, Fun Running: Have the girls do core work both standing and on the floor. Begin with the importance of strengthening this part of their bodies. "Your core holds you up all day long so it's important to exercise it in the correct way," tell them. "We can do this by standing up and working it and by exercising on the floor. Core means your middle, both belly and back and all the muscles that support the middle of your body."

Standing Oblique Crunches: While standing up tall, shoulders back and chest open, place your feet shoulder distance apart. Bring your left knee to your right elbow by lifting it across your body. Do 10 on one side and 10 on the other. When you switch sides it will be right knee to left elbow.

Forward Bends with Lower Back Lifts: Counter stretch/exercise for the back. Lift your hands over your head and reach for the sky. You are long and tall with extension. Begin to roll forward keeping your back soft as you bend towards the floor. Hang like a rag doll. Feel the stretch. Straighten your back, tailbone towards the ceiling, belly button drawn in and begin to lift. Be gentle and strong. Hold for a 10-count when parallel to the floor. Relax your back, round your shoulders and repeat 3 times.

Standing Twists: Stand with your shoulders back and chest open, feet slightly more than shoulder width apart. Arms are tucked in along your side with elbows bent and knuckles facing the ceiling (sky). Hands are in a fist. Keeping your hips facing forward and abdominal muscles engaged twist from side to side. Be strong and resist in both directions. Feel the burn! Do for 30 seconds. Do 2 sets.

Accordion: Have the girls hit the floor and sit on their buns. Have them lean slightly back and feel their tummies engage. Talk about it, have them feel it. Then with knees bent they should try to lift their legs. Ankles and knees stay together. Hands are on the ground on either side of their bodies to keep them balanced. They should then sit up and bring the knees in for a squeeze then release with knees back to starting position. Repeat this in and out motion for a 10-count. Then have them try to do a 20-count. Talk about the challenge but also how daily doses of exercise will make them strong and fabulous!

Boot Camp: Set up flat targets, low profile cones, hula hoops, and jump ropes. Put on the music and have the girls go through an obstacle course. Be creative! While they are doing this have them freeze and give you 20 jumping jacks or 20 mountain climbers to keep it fun and interesting.

Fun Running: Put everyone on one wall and have them run on your whistle. One whistle is run, two is freeze. See who has on their listening ears. Then change it up or add a third whistle:

- 1 = run,
- 2 = freeze,
- 3 = walk,

- 4 = skip,
- 5 = hop on one foot.

Have fun with this, the girls love it! This is great to do at the end of class to get them focused, and have them do lots of "I Am" statements here. Get them fired up before they leave you for the week.

Include "I Am" Statements: Ask for volunteers to give words.

PART 5: WRAP UP

Class Commencement: Have the girls come back together in a group. Give them some positive feedback from the class. Remind them to "pay it forward" when they see an opportunity, to be kind or do something nice for someone for no reason.

Verbally Assign Homework: The girls should do something kind and loving for someone this week. Perhaps let a sibling win when they are having an argument or invite someone that doesn't normally sit with them at lunch to join them. The girls should be prepared to discuss what they did next week.

Greet Parents: Greet the parents as they come for pick-up and answer any questions they have. Positive energy and friendliness go a long way!

EQUIPMENT AND MATERIALS

- Jump ropes
- Hula hoops
- Low-profile cones
- Flat targets
- Whistle
- Marker/pencil bin
- Scrapbook pages or card stock
- Glue sticks
- Scissors
- Stickers

POSITIVE THOUGHTS

FOR THE WEEK AND BEYOND!

Strong body, strong mind, strong YOU!

Being kind to others shows how strong you are inside and out!

Do one kind thing every day for someone you care about.

Being kind to others makes you feel great about yourself!

The greatest gift in life is love. Love yourself, love your family, and love your friends!

Food for thought: Once you say something and the words leave your lips, you can't take them back! Think before you speak.

BACKGROUND AND THEORY

MORE BEES WITH HONEY

WE DO A WHOLE CLASS on love and kindness and it's kind of a paying it forward lesson plan. There are different kinds of random acts of kindness where you either keep it to yourself because it feels good in your heart, or you're doing something kind and giving in an outward way, like running a race for charity, and we discuss both. My niece Gabrielle is taking it to a whole new level. She's part of what's called the Angel Fund, which raises funds and awareness in an effort to find a cure for ALS. She's taken it upon herself to do this charitable work by setting up a web page once a year and sharing what she's doing with others. She has done this for at least four or five years now and she's only a teenager! She already knows at this young age how good it feels to do things that help others. At a very young age she was getting that feeling of "Wow! I can have a positive impact on people! I can help worthy causes and all of that stuff! I can give to this community, to this school or to this organization!"

And speaking of Gaby, I can tell you exactly where the Love and Kindness class came from. Part of my strategy when I was thinking of how to help Gaby with the girls that were picking on her on the school bus, was that I really wanted her to stick up for herself in a way that she could later feel proud of. I wanted her to also be loving and kind. I wanted to give her the tools that would help her rise above the "mean girls," maybe even inspire them to be more kind and loving themselves. I believe that sometimes neither kids nor adults take a minute to come to a loving place with themselves or others. For example, let's say someone is grouchy in the grocery store. Well, maybe they just lost someone that they love? Who knows?

I think the world would be a better place if we all came from a place of loving kindness. Giving others some grace, cutting each other some slack, and first assuming the best in others versus the worst, would all go a long way. So with Gaby, although she certainly wasn't in a place yet to love these girls who were not being nice to her, she could be kind in how she handled the situation. I wanted to teach her to always be kind. She does that and now we have taught hundreds, maybe thousands of other girls to do that too!

MEAN GIRLS

Mean girls come in every age, unfortunately. But I believe that by teaching girls at a young age about love and kindness chances are better that they will go about life in a more open, positive, and kind way. By teaching girls how good it can feel to be kind or do the right thing they will want to experience that more, versus feeling terrible for being mean, unkind, or insecure. The reality is that when we are mean or unkind we never feel good afterwards and we never get what we want in the end. Knowing this or experiencing it first-hand reminds and solidifies that being loving and kind is always the best approach, even in difficult times or situations. Many times doing the right thing is not easy but it always feels the best!

So I teach the girls to assume the best in others, to be kind to themselves and everyone they meet. Know that you have the power to choose who you want to be, how you want to show up and with whom you want to "do the dance" with. What does that mean, "doing the dance?" It's a phrase I like to use and what it means to me is that when you are "doing the dance," you are harmonious, aligned, and feel really good when you are with those people. When you are "doing the dance" with others you are able to be your best self and let your light shine bright!

I teach girls to be kind to all people as we never know what someone else might be facing or going through. Always assume the best in others and offer the best "you" that you can. Girls "get it" when we discuss love and kindness and they often leave class looking for ways that they can make others feel good, special, or valued. And that's pretty cool!

THE MEAN GIRL

Now, dear reader, are you sitting down? I think *I* was that mean girl. Actually I know that I was the mean girl at times— not always but sometimes. I was the mean girl on the bus and I don't want girls to be like that! Maybe that's part of why I do what I do in this program for girls. I want girls to learn to be amazing to each other. There was a girl I picked on over and over and it was because I wasn't standing in my power. I was insecure and wanted attention. I was ten years old. My mom taught me that I could do better, that I could be the girl that *protected* others, and by the end of middle school I was! I knew being mean didn't feel good deep down so I changed. It's that simple but it takes practice and patience. I'm a big believer that you are what you think. We're going to make mistakes but if we learn from them and do our best to do better, that's enough. You can't do better than your best, right? Always be striving to do better.

These lessons are easier said than done of course. Sometimes girls will have a little tiff right in my class and I'm like, "Whoa, whoa! We need to talk about that! What just happened?" They usually don't want to talk about it—one of them is embarrassed, one cries, and it gets a little hairy. But 99 percent of the time I can get whoever the girl was who did something hurtful to realize that "We're not mad at you and no one hates you."

"Oh, *everyone* hates me!" she might say.

"Well, no," I say, "but can you see how you could have done better? How could you have expressed your feelings in a way that was not hurtful? Perhaps in a kind or gentle way?"

These situations are also opportunities for girls to practice forgiveness. Maybe one girl took something from another girl or said something mean. Whatever it was, we talk it through. I ask them, "How could you have done that better? Maybe you could have asked for help from me if you girls couldn't work it out together? Maybe you could have compromised?" After we discuss it I assure them that the next time they will make good choices. I'm always proud of them when we have these uncomfortable discussions. I assure them it's not always easy to express our feelings, especially if we feel wronged in some way or we just want to be right. These are teachable moments, they're all opportunities to grow.

That's a big part of Girl Power, teaching girls it's okay to make mistakes, to learn from them, take responsibility for your actions, and learn how to handle it better in the future.

Forgive yourself and move on because that will make you awesome! If you do everything right all the time, where do you go from there? We need to teach and experience love and kindness wherever we can, and when we realize how great it feels, we happily pay it forward.

MY OWN LOVE AND KINDNESS BREAKTHROUGH

So I've learned this—the usefulness of love and kindness—myself. My sister Michelle and I were super-super close and we're each other's biggest cheerleaders, but we're also very different, and we still have conflicts at times. It's normal and we are no different than most. Siblings have conflicts, even in adult life. At some point I realized that a lot of our conflict was because she was always trying to take care of me in the most loving way. She's my older sister, my only sister. We grew up together with only our mother. Then my mom died very unexpectedly. So in my sister's eyes, I'm always the youngest. I'm always that person that she needs to take care of and it was the craziest thing—all of the sudden it was just the two of us to take care of one another.

When I really started to think about this I thought, "Why can't I sort this out?" And I realized she's telling me what to do not because she thinks I can't do it on my own, or because I don't know something, or because I'm not strong enough, but rather she's telling me because she wants to take care of me, in a really loving and kind way. I'm so grateful for that and for her. I know my mother is smiling down probably saying, "It's about time!"

And now, we don't have those conflicts anymore. She doesn't even know, we haven't talked about it, but I made a conscious decision to say, "You know what? Michelle, when we have this dynamic that we have had our whole lives, I'm going to start to take a deep breath, and I'm going to ask myself 'What is this place? Where is she coming from?'" And if I can be sensitive to where that other person is coming from, it makes it easy to not be right, to not have to debate. All that other stuff just kind of melts away, because now I'm open to listening.

I can still do things my way, where before I was taking it almost as an insult. "Doesn't she know I'm an adult? You know, I'm a big girl!" But then I realized she is always coming from a place of protection and love, whether she even knows that or not. And now it's like magic.

CHECKING IN

When you don't handle things with love and kindness potential friendships and lessons might be missed or never be realized, and someone might get hurt. Actions always speak louder than words, so make your actions count and make them ones you will be proud of. I do talk to the girls in my classes about social media and protecting themselves, but also about this love and kindness stuff, and how once it comes out of your mouth you can't take it back, so show up in a way that you feel good about. When we are discussing social media I try to give the girls ways to "check in with themselves" regarding the things they *say*. One way that I do this is by telling them about what I call the "Three P's"—your parents, your principal, and your priest or pastor.

I teach the girls to also check in with what they are *doing* whether it's with pictures, text, or words. If you wouldn't take those actions or say those things in front of those three P's, your parents, principle, and your priest/pastor, then you probably shouldn't do them. It kind of keeps you in check. I'm teaching kids to say, "I need to check in with myself for a minute. How do I want to handle this?"

People are so reactive, they are often not acting, they are reacting. It makes a huge difference. In a middle school, for example, I will touch on all of these topics, depending on how the flow of the class goes. I am reiterating that to all the kids I work with all the time. I would say it's a golden rule and they get it. I ask them directly, if they have a phone, if they showed me their phone what would I see and would they be proud of it or embarrassed? They actually don't need to say a thing after that I as can read their reactions and faces pretty easily! It's not rocket science to know who's behaving and who's pushing the envelope here.

CLASS #6: HEALTHY EATING HABITS THAT LAST A LIFETIME

IN THIS CHAPTER

CLASS ORGANIZATION

AND MATERIALS

- Part 1: Welcome and Warm Up
- Part 2: Discussion
- Part 3: Activities
- Part 4: Fitness
- Part 5: Wrap Up
- Equipment and Materials
- Favorite Fruits and Veggies Worksheet
- Healthy Snacking Tips
- Food Challenge Chart
- Positive Thoughts

BACKGROUND

AND THEORY

- Good Food is Power
- The Family Food Challenge
- Rethink Your Drink
- Hydration
- Awesome Tips and Healthy Snacks
- The Spice of Life

CLASS ORGANIZATION AND MATERIALS

PART 1: WELCOME AND WARM UP

Get the Group Moving: Have the group spread out and warm them up with dynamic stretching, jumping jacks, running in place or laps around the room, then static stretching. Do these for 3-5 minutes to warm them up and help them burn some nervous/excited energy.

Review Homework: If homework was assigned the previous class, go over it together. Encourage the girls to share with the rest of the group.

PART 2: DISCUSSION

Food as Fuel: Help the girls to view *food as fuel* and educate them on how to make healthy food choices throughout the day. Have the girls gather after the warm-up and begin to discuss how they currently view food. Why do we eat? What does food do for our bodies? How do we feel after we eat? What kinds of things are they eating? Let the girls share their favorite foods as well as their least favorite foods. Educate the girls on the importance of healthy foods in their lives, and how fruits, vegetables, nuts, grains, dairy and water all have important roles in a balanced diet and healthy lifestyle.

Give examples:

- If you put good things in, you get good things out!
- Strong bodies are the result of healthy eating.
- Healthy snacking helps kids to run faster and play harder for a longer period of time.
- Your brain works better when it has healthy levels of nutrients. You can solve problems more efficiently and do better in school with a balanced diet.

Talk about the importance of breakfast. Breakfast really *is* the most important meal of the day. It gets your metabolism going. It fires your body up for the day and helps you to feel strong and fabulous! Ask what they eat for breakfast. If they don't eat breakfast ask why. Encourage the girls to share what their eating habits are and how they view food. Explain that food is fuel to their bodies as gas is to our cars. It will take them places but only so far if they don't fill their tanks with good nutritious foods throughout the day.

When it comes to snacking teach the girls to have something healthy first. If they are still hungry then have a salty, crunchy, or sweet treat. Planning ahead is key when kids are playing sports or rushing to music lessons, dance lessons or hanging out with their friends. Review the Healthy Eating Tips handout. Let the girls share what they typically snack on when they are going from one activity to another.

<u>Fueling for Sports Discussion</u>: Educate the girls on how to get the most out of their bodies when playing sports. Hydrate, hydrate, hydrate with water. If you prefer sports drinks water them down. Most sports drinks contain way too much sugar and contain 2 to 2.5 servings in one bottle, therefore many more calories and much more sugar than you

might realize. Cut the sugar and calorie content by adding water to your sports drinks. Same electrolyte benefits with half the sugar and calories!

Healthy Snacking Options:

- Plain water with a banana is great fuel!
- Greek or regular yogurt and a handful of almonds or walnuts post workout/training is a great recovery combination.
- Apple with peanut or sun butter.
- Carrots, cucumbers, grapes and pretzels are all easy to pack and take with you.

PART 3: ACTIVITIES

Favorite Fruits and Veggies Worksheet: Each girl gets the following materials:

- Favorite Fruits and Veggies printout
- Community use of markers/pencils

Have the girls fill out and decorate their sheets with their favorite fruits and vegetables. Once they have all completed their pages, encourage them to share what they have written down. See how many girls like and dislike the same things. How many green veggies did they come up with? Who likes orange and red fruits or veggies? Encourage the girls to mix it up this week and try something that they haven't liked in the past. You will talk about it next week.

Meanwhile, talk about how a variety of choices is a great idea and to try to get as many different colored fruits and vegetables into their daily eating as possible.

<u>Healthy Food Chart Challenge:</u> Each girl gets the following materials:

- Poster board
- Paper ruler
- Community use of the markers/pencils

Instruct the girls to make a food chart that they will use this week to do a healthy food challenge with their families. First, have each girl make a horizontal line for each family member in their household. Show them your example and assist them if needed. Then, have the girls do a column from top to bottom for every day of the week starting tomorrow.

For example, if your class meets on Thursday afternoons they should start the week on their chart with Friday. If your class meets on Tuesday they should make the first column on their chart Wednesday. After the rows and columns have been created they should put the days of the week across the top putting one day in each column. Then have them list each family member beginning with herself at the top and listing them from top to bottom. Lastly, they should put circles in the far right box on the last day of the challenge for each participant. This circle is where they will put the totals for the week.

Now that the chart is made they may decorate it. They should track the weekly total for each person. Every time someone in the house has a fruit or veggie they earn a tally mark on the chart. At the end of the week add up the tally marks. The person with the most tally marks for healthy foods on the chart might win a prize in their house or get to pick a family activity. Encourage the girls to make it fun! The girls should bring their chart back to class next week.

Discuss serving sizes. Here are some examples:

- A cup of grapes versus a single grape.
- Orange and apple juice can be counted as servings of fruit as they have natural sugar. 8oz. is one serving.
- Servings of salad are tallied by the cup. You may *not* count each fruit or veggie in the salad as a tally mark.

Clean Up: Have the group pick up all the supplies and throw away any trash.

PART 4: FITNESS

Circle to Circle: Have the girls form a large circle holding hands. Explain to them that they are like a chain conducting an electrical current. Have one girl start by lifting her hand which brings up the hand of the next girl in the chain or circle. They should continue all the way around the circle. This gives them a sense or feeling of being connected to each other. Once they get the "current" to travel around the circle a few times, disconnect one set of girl's hands. Add a hula hoop and reconnect them. The game just got more fun and slightly complicated!

Give the girls instructions that the purpose is to work together and get the hula hoop all the way around the circle without breaking the chain. They will have to work together to maneuver the hula hoop over and around each girl in the chain.

If there is time blindfold one of the girls and have them do it again with the hula hoop working as a team to guide the girl that has lost her vision with the blindfold.

Include "I Am" Statements:

- "I am a team player!"
- "I am connected!"
- "I am a problem solver!"
- "I am smart!"

Ask for volunteers to give other words that will inspire and motivate them to work together.

PART 5: WRAP UP

Class Commencement: Have the girls come back together in a group. Give them some positive feedback from the class. Remind them to make healthy food choices to keep themselves feeling fabulous and energized.

Verbally Assign Homework: The girls should use the food chart that they created in class to mark down how many fruits and how many vegetables they eat each day for the week. They should challenge their families to eat healthy this week as well. Remind them that it is a "Family Healthy Eating Challenge."

Greet Parents: Greet the parents as they come for pick-up and answer any questions they have. Positive energy and friendliness go a long way! Mention the Healthy Food

Challenge assignment and let parents know that a little "healthy" competition is often a great way to get kids to eat healthier!

EQUIPMENT AND MATERIALS

- Hula hoops
- Marker/pencil bin
- Favorite Fruits and Vegetables Worksheet
- Poster board
- Paper ruler
- Healthy Eating Tips handout

FAVORITE FRUITS AND VEGGIES WORKSHEET

List your top 3 favorite veggies:

1.) _____

2.) _____

3.) _____

List your top 3 favorite fruits:

1.) _____

2.) _____

3.) _____

HEALTHY SNACKING TIPS

Always try to have something healthy first. If you are still hungry then have a treat—something sweet, crunchy or salty.

- Good "starters" would be apples, oranges, a banana, celery with peanut or soy butter, carrots, raw green beans or snap peas, grapes, berries, yogurt.
- All of these healthy snacks are easy to pack and travel with. They are great for energy before sports and will nourish your body while you exercise and play!

Still hungry? Enjoy any of the following crunchy, slightly salty, or sweet snacks that are still low in sugar but satisfy.

- Homemade Brown Rice Tortilla Chips or air popcorn
- Pretzels
- Fruit kabobs with mini marshmallow's and your favorite fruits

FOOD CHALLENGE CHART

List the days of the week across the top of the chart beginning with the first day that you begin the challenge. For example, If class meets on Tuesday the first day of the chart should be Wednesday. After completing the challenge for the week bring it back to school with you for our next class. It's fun to review and compare with your classmates.

List the members of your family from top to bottom. List the weekly totals in the bottom right corner on the last day of the challenge.

Every time someone has a serving for fruits or vegetables track it on their row on the day of the week with a tally mark. Track healthy servings all week. The person in your family with the most- healthy servings at the end of the week wins!

Make it fun. You might have the winner pick a family activity to do together after the challenge. Things that other families have done in the past include the winner picks a movie to go to or dinner at their favorite restaurant. Good luck and enjoy the healthy eating!

An example of what your chart might look like is on the next page:

"HEALTHY COMPETITION" FOOD CHALLENGE CHART

Family Member	Wednesday	Thursday	Friday	Saturday	Sunday	Monday	Tuesday	Totals
Robby								
Kayla								
Mom								
Dad								

You have ONE body, take care of it!

Exercise and healthy eating give you the power and focus to do AMAZING things!

What you put in is what you get out, so put healthy foods in and get amazing results out!

Know that your body is changing but it is just as it should be right now! Love every stage!

BACKGROUND AND THEORY

GOOD FOOD IS POWER

MY KIDS EAT things like grapes, apples, and cucumbers as snacks. They are healthy eaters no doubt, because I have been feeding them that way their entire lives. Sometimes I get push-back but they are *kids,* I get it! The good news is kids, like all people, can develop their tastes as they improve their nutrition and daily diet. They can lose their interest or cravings for sugar and fried, fatty foods. If they don't take to cucumbers, apples, grapes and other healthy snacks right away, don't worry. Just put them on a gradual runway and you can improve their nutrition.

In my Healthy Eating class we used to do a taste testing but nowadays there are so many allergies around it's trickier to do. I would have them taste and compare all sorts of foods—salty, crunchy, sweet. We would discuss preferences and what they snack on in their homes. And I have heard it *all* in this class! I teach the kids about healthy options and help them to see and understand that food is fuel to our bodies just like gasoline is to a car. I ask them questions like, "If you had some Oreos and some Doritos on your way to soccer, how long would you be able to run around?" They actually often find that question silly.

"Oh gosh," they'll say, "I'd be out of steam in no time!"

So then I'll ask them, "Well, what if you had an apple with some SunButter or almond butter?"

We use SunButter in my house because my son has allergies to peanuts and tree nuts. Sunflower seed butter is another great alternative for families that have children with nut allergies and it tastes amazing! So I teach them to always try to have something healthy first and then if they are still hungry, go for something crunchy, salty, or sweet. We do enjoy those things in our diets, but it's best not to start with them. Or better yet, get the crunchy fix from things like celery or carrots and your sweet from fruits.

When I work with middle school girls, I impress upon them the importance of fueling their bodies properly. Middle school is often when and where many girls develop eating disorders and an unhealthy self-body image. That is why this is a critical place for me to connect with the girls regarding their nutrition. I teach them that they need to eat well and they need to eat enough. I teach them that in order to have a strong, healthy body they need to fuel their bodies on a

131

regular basis. That means balanced meals and snacks packed with nourishment. We discuss "empty" calories and how they don't serve their bodies. I give girls examples that are easy to understand and relatable. For instance, I ask the girls, "If you have a car and it takes unleaded fuel to run its best, how would it run if you put diesel fuel in the tank?"

"Not very well!" they say.

"Correct!"

And we discuss how fueling your car *is* the same as fueling your body. If you don't put in good fuel, meaning the proper balance of lean protein, healthy carbohydrates, and healthy fats, your body won't run efficiently. Just like the car that has the wrong gas or fuel. In order to run faster, play harder, get good grades, sleep well, and have overall good health, girls need to learn and practice proper nutrition. And we teach that in Girl Power! If I can get them to shift their thinking and look at food as fuel as well as the benefits of a strong, healthy body, then it's harder for them to go into a dark place where they deprive themselves or binge eat.

I teach a girl to love her body at every stage and to take good care of it as it's the only one she's got and it's forever! I start to lay the brickwork for them to love food and realize that just because a food is healthy doesn't mean it won't taste awesome or satisfy. I teach them that you can have some greens and some beautiful vegetables and fruits, and it's also okay to have pizza. The key is balance. I educate girls on balanced nutrition and how to love foods while loving their bodies. I want girls to learn about eating for power— powerful minds, powerful bodies, powerful girls! We discuss foods that are packed with vitamins and minerals, things that are "packed with power," as I always tell them, and it's all about *power! Girl power!*

THE FAMILY FOOD CHALLENGE

I love getting emails from parents and always look forward to hearing how the kids are more open-minded about healthy eating after leaving this class. I do a lot of different activities in the classes and one of them that has become really popular with the girls and their families (that I also love) is the food chart activity. A mom sent me an email. Her daughter was taking my Girl Power class and she had an older sister. The mom told me that for the first time ever in their home her daughters were eating salads and talking about healthy foods. She thanked me for giving them a fun and healthy way of looking at food and healthy eating.

I'll bring in a bunch of poster boards and we make a food chart together. The food chart has their names and the names of their family members on it. We also put the days of the week across the top of the chart. It becomes a grid to track healthy servings for the week for the entire family. I then challenge them to challenge their families at home to eat healthy for a whole week. They get a tally mark for every healthy serving and we talk about what a serving looks like. For example, I show them that a serving of salad is about the size of a tennis ball, or depending on how old they are, it might be the size of their fist. This gives the girls a clear picture of a serving and they love giving themselves credit for healthy eating.

When I explain the challenge I suggest that they set up a "prize." They might decide that at the end of the week whoever wins gets to decide on a family activity together. Or maybe they will go to a movie together or their favorite family restaurant. They might cook a meal together or go do something active. Whatever you do, make it fun. This creates an incentive. The hope is that everyone wants in on the fun while also eating healthy. At times they don't even realize they are eating healthier all week long!

I'm always excited to hear how the girls and their families did with the challenge. Kids are so funny—they will say things to me like, "Oh, my dad will lose because he is the worst eater! He eats fast food all the time." Or they might say, "My mother eats so healthy but I beat her this week!" They feel so proud of themselves and often bring their charts back in to share with me. I love seeing the charts and talking with the girls about their success. They'll tell me how they had more energy and how they feel more powerful when they are eating healthy.

RETHINK YOUR DRINK

Within the nutrition class I do a spin off class that I call "Rethink Your Drink." Now, you may have heard something like that before—I know Nike does a whole campaign called, "Rethink Your Drink"—but what I try to do for this class is get the girls really thinking about what they are drinking. I ask them what three or four of their favorite drinks are, and what might they drink for fuel on the soccer field or before they go to play ice hockey or go to a dance class. I ask them how to they hydrate to play hard. A lot of kids do say water, but many kids will say sports drinks.

I teach the girls how to read the labels on these drinks and we do a comparison and tasting in class. Knowledge is power and when the girls learn how much sugar is in many of these sports drinks they decide they are not the best fuel for sports at all. There's a lot of sugar in these drinks! Now, many studies have been done about whether sports drinks are appropriate for kids or not. Certainly if a child is doing strenuous activity in the blazing sun all weekend during a soccer or lacrosse tournament it can be difficult to stay hydrated. In those cases a sports drink may help with hydration because of the electrolytes and sodium. However, for moderate physical activity or exercise water is the best drink to stay hydrated, especially for kids!

With that said I like kids to learn this on many levels. I teach them how to read the labels and we do a little math. Typically when the serving size is 2.5 servings per bottle it's easy to confuse the consumer. Parents and kids alike can sometimes misunderstand the total calories and sugar content. For example, one 12-ounce bottle of Gatorade Thirst Quench has 21 grams of sugar. However, their regular bottle contains 32 ounces, which means it packs *56 grams of sugar*. The daily recommended sugar intake for a child is 4 teaspoons or just 16 grams! For a teenager the recommended daily intake of sugar is 5 to 8 teaspoons or 20 to 32 grams. In both cases you can see how these sports drinks contain way too much sugar and calories from sugar for our kids.

After I teach the girls how to understand the labels we begin tasting and then building our sugar towers. Prior to this class I asked them what their favorite drinks were, so for the

Healthy Eating class I can bring in an assortment of these drinks and some Dixie cups so we can all try samples. Before we start I set a timer and I tell them all, "At some point during this class one of you is going to make a statement, and when you do I will tell you how long it took."

Inevitably, it always happens in this class that one of the girls will at some point say, "Mrs. Mahoney, I am never going to have that sports drink again!"

It always makes me so happy. I give them some tools and educate them on reading labels, and *boom*—they learn and they decide it's not healthy, it's not good enough for their bodies. This is very different from a parent or teacher saying something like "Don't drink that, it's bad for you," or "It has too much sugar." Letting the kids learn, see, and decide for themselves is so much more powerful! So they learn to read labels and taste different favorites. They can then go off and make educated decisions!

I bring sugar cubes to this class for the visual portion of the lesson. I show and explain to the girls that I have brought in sugar cubes for the purpose of getting a clear picture of how much sugar is in each of the drinks we are tasting and learning about. In a tiny sugar cube there are two grams of sugar. So what I have the kids do is by using sugar cubes, show me the amount of sugar in each drink. They'll build towers and create shapes on the paper plates. They are shocked at how many sugar cubes I hand out for each of the drink's equivalent sugar content. And then it happens—they *really* see and realize how much sugar is actually in those drinks. And that's when *they* decide they don't want to drink them anymore. It's awesome because I know they have learned a powerful lesson—how to make a decision based on taking good care of their bodies and their health. I just showed them what was in some of the drinks they may have been consuming. When they had the facts, they wanted to make healthy decisions. Pure awesomeness! The girls love, love, love this class every time I teach it, regardless of their age.

When parents or guardians arrive to pick the girls up, the girls always want to rush over to show them what they have learned. They show them their sugar towers and explain their meaning. They might also say something like, "I'm not drinking sports drinks anymore! They have way too much sugar!" And here's a tip for parents: Water down the sugary sports drinks! Your kids will get used to the flavor and may even like it better. They will consume a fraction of the sugar and still enjoy something with flavor as they stay hydrated.

HYDRATION

And we do also talk with the girls about the importance of staying hydrated. I teach them that when you're thirsty you are actually already dehydrated so try to drink enough, enough so you never really feel thirsty. Once you feel thirsty it's difficult to catch up on the water, the hydration you need. Whether they are playing on the playground or playing sports they love, I tell kids to drink more water than you think you need. Drink it *before* sports, before you're active. Drink water *while* you're active if possible, and you need to drink water *after* you're active for recovery. Water, water, water!

We want to teach kids, whether they are active on the playground or on the lacrosse field, where they are running around for an extended period on a hot day, they need to make sure they have their water. They need to have it in their lunch, and if it's allowed in your child's school, encourage them to have a water bottle at their desk throughout the school day.

AWESOME TIPS AND HEALTHY SNACKS

I try to give both kids and parents little tricks to help them eat healthier. Vegetables can be fantastic as snacks—carrot sticks, celery with SunButter or a green apple and some almonds are very good options. These snacks are great on the way to a sport or from one activity to another. Maybe you are going from school to a music lesson. You will need to concentrate and proper nutrition will help. I call these "grab and go snacks." It's great to have things that you can just take with you on the run.

Taco night can be both fun and healthy. Add lots of veggies and let the kids put together their own tacos. I teach parents how to bury vegetables into sauces and homemade pizza. Making it fun for your kids is half the battle. I teach parents to never say things like, "This is so healthy you will love it!" because that's the best way to get your kids to *not* eat it! What kids really need are foods that are actually going to give them fuel all day long, so we want to be sure that that we're providing our kids with nutritional balance most of all.

I always encourage girls to try some new food, at least once a week. I'll tell them to try something this week that they have never liked or haven't tried before, and they may need to be brave and courageous here! Maybe that's cucumbers, for example. It is true that our taste buds change, which means that our preferences change. For example, I know that I never loved broccoli as a kid but now I do! So one big tip I always give girls with food is to never count it out. You might have hated green beans in second grade but in the fourth grade you might love them. An open mind to new things—even food—is a powerful thing!

THE SPICE OF LIFE

In my nutrition class we also make *fruit* kebabs. We talk about the kebabs as the girls make patterns out of strawberries and grapes for them. Just before the girls are done I break out some mini marshmallows. We talk about balance. I will say, "If I put these marshmallows out earlier maybe you would have made a whole skewer of marshmallows, but how would that have fueled you?"

"It wouldn't fuel us Mrs. Mahoney!" they will say.

But if we put the marshmallows on last, they might remove a few strawberries or rearrange the pattern so every fourth or fifth bite you have something sweet. This is also a very visual exercise for kids and they love it. They get it, and it gets them talking and thinking about healthier choices and ways to snack for fueling their bodies. If they have all this healthy food out would they even want the marshmallows at the end? They might not. A lot of times they don't. "Oh, Mrs. Mahoney, mine is already built. I'm good," they say.

And that's the lesson right there—if we can educate our kids, make them part of the discussion regarding healthy eating, show them visuals that empower them, and then give them the opportunity to choose, they are likely to make good decisions. I have seen it. Empowered girls are smart girls! I believe if we teach kids to look at food as fuel and their bodies as well-oiled machines then we are steering them in the right direction!

~

This is (another) one of my favorite classes as the kids can really relate. It's visual and empowering. I teach the girls that they have the power to make good decisions for their bodies even at a young age. I give them the information and always love that by the end of this class *they* see and want to make healthy choices!

CLASS #7: THE IMPORTANCE OF REST

IN THIS CHAPTER

CLASS ORGANIZATION AND MATERIALS	BACKGROUND AND THEORY

CLASS ORGANIZATION AND MATERIALS

- Part 1: Welcome and Warm Up
- Part 2: Discussion
- Part 3: Activities
- Part 4: Fitness/Yoga
- Part 5: Hand Outs and Wrap Up
- Equipment and Materials
- Sleep Pattern Worksheet
- Positive Thoughts

BACKGROUND AND THEORY

- Food and Sleep

CLASS ORGANIZATION AND MATERIALS

PART 1: WELCOME AND WARM UP

<u>Get the Group Moving:</u> Have the group spread out and warm them up with dynamic and static stretching to prepare them for yoga. Do this for 5-10 minutes to warm them up. Then call the group to sit in front of you.

<u>Review Homework:</u> If homework was assigned in the previous class, go over it together. Encourage the girls to share what they did with the rest of the group.

PART 2: DISCUSSION

<u>Sleep Pattern Discussion</u>: Get the girls talking about their bedtime routines. What time do they go to sleep at night? Is it different on school nights versus weekends? Ask with a show of hands how many girls go to be at 7:30, 8, 8:30, 9, 9:30 or later on school nights. Ask if they do anything to "settle down" on a regular basis. Examples might be that they read before bed either alone or with a parent, take a relaxing bath, or play a quiet game. After discussing the bedtime routine talk with the girls about their morning or wake-up routines. How many girls wake up at 6, 6:30, 7, 7:30 and so on.

Let the girls share what their bedtimes and wake-up times are as well at their before bed routines. Talk about the importance of slowing down at night to transition to sleep. This week they should try to establish a relaxing bedtime routine. This is part of their homework for the week.

Educate the girls on the proper amount of sleep that they should be getting. The following are accepted standards for sleep in children:

- "Children 6 to 12 years of age should sleep 9 to 12 hours per 24 hours on a regular basis to promote optimal health.
- "Teenagers 13 to 18 years of age should sleep 8 to 10 hours per 24 hours on a regular basis to promote optimal health.

"The group found that adequate sleep duration for age on a regular basis leads to improved attention, behavior, learning, memory, emotional regulation, quality of life, and mental and physical health. Not getting enough sleep each night is associated with an increase in injuries, hypertension, obesity and depression . . ."[12]

The proper amount of rest is critical for children as they develop and grow while they sleep. Brain function and musculoskeletal (muscles and bones) growth takes place when

---

[12] https://www.aap.org/en-us/about-the-aap/aap-press-room/pages/American-Academy-of-Pediatrics-Supports-Childhood-Sleep-Guidelines.aspx

the body is at rest, therefore proper rest in children is an absolute must for healthy active kids.

Encourage the girls to monitor their sleep patterns this week and give the Feeling Faces handout so that they can track how they feel with and without proper sleep.

PART 3: ACTIVITIES

Pillow Cases: Each girl gets the following materials:

- Pillowcase
- Community use of fabric markers
- One Sheet of poster board to slip inside the pillowcase while they are working. This will prevent markers from bleeding through and allow the girls to decorate both sides.

Have the girls decorate their pillowcase however they would like. Once they have all completed their projects, encourage them to share what they have created.

Clean Up: Have the group help pick up all the supplies and throw away any trash.

Or (alternate exercise), Book Mark Activity: Each girl gets the following materials:

- Bookmark
- Community use of markers/pencils
- Stickers

Have the girls decorate their bookmarks however they would like. Once they have all completed their projects, encourage them to share what they have created.

Clean Up: Have the group help pick up all the supplies and throw away any trash.

Or (alternate exercise), Night Shirt Activity: Each girl gets the following materials:

- T-shirt
- One Sheet of poster board to slip inside T-shirt while they are working. This will prevent markers from bleeding through and allow the girls to decorate both sides.
- Community use of fabric markers

Have the girls decorate their T-shirts however they would like. Once they have all completed their projects, encourage them to share what they have created.

Clean Up: Have the group help pick up all the supplies and throw away any trash.

PART 4: FITNESS/YOGA

Yoga: Have the girls spread out and remove their shoes. Begin with standing postures/asanas (poses). Walk the girls through the yoga practice with a lot of verbal queues. Be sure they are being safe and always protecting their joints and back.

The routine will begin with standing postures moving into balance postures. Bending poses are very nourishing and should be done at the end before rest. You can move the girls through a basic flow of multiple postures by following the sequence below. The class concludes with relaxation and meditative or rest postures.

Note: When teaching yoga to kids keep in mind that children might not be able to hold yoga poses as long as adults and their naturally short attention spans might be a challenge; however there are many benefits to yoga for kids. It can help develop their bodies, brains, self-esteem and emotional health. Yoga can also help kids cope with stress and sharpen their awareness. It can help them become more creative and calm. Be sure when you are teaching yoga to kids to keep safe, fun and simple.

Teach the following asanas.

STANDING AND STRENGTH POSES

Mountain Pose (Tadasana) has you mimic a mountain by standing tall and steady. This is a basic starting pose for many standing poses in yoga. Have the girls focus on grounding their feet into the floor and the top of their heads reaching through the ceiling. Shoulders back, chest open with good posture and breath.

Warrior I (Virabhadrasana I) is a focusing and strengthening pose, meant to build a connection, grounding you with the Earth's energy. Start standing in Mountain Pose. Jump your feet out or step them out. Place your hands on your hips and turn your right leg and foot out by 90 degrees. Your right heel should be directly opposite the inner arch of your left foot. Turn your left leg and foot in by about 45 degrees. Take a moment to make sure you are balanced, focusing your attention on the floor beneath you. Turn your chest to the right. Press your left hip forward in order to square your hips. On your next inhale, raise your arms above your head and bring your palms together. Gaze straight ahead and focus on the power of the pose. Exhale and bend your right knee to a 90-degree angle. Your knee should be right over your ankle.

Take a moment to balance your body, pressing your weight into your right thigh. As you drop your tailbone down towards the floor, opening the front of the hips and the pelvic abdomen, lean your head back and gaze upwards at your fingertips. Stretch upwards through your middle back and arms. Hold this pose for five breaths. Inhale and straighten your legs. Lower your arms and bring your legs together again to return to Mountain Pose.

Repeat to the other side.

Warrior II (Virabhadrasana II) is meant as a powerful pose to connect our legs to action. Tell the girls to feel the power coursing through them as they do this pose. Start standing in Mountain Pose. Step or jump your feet wide across the mat. Turn your left foot out by 90 degrees. The heel should be just opposite your right arch. Turn your right foot in slightly. Raise your arms to the sides. Make sure you keep your shoulders down while your palms face the ground. Rest your gaze on the very tips of your left fingers as you extend out through your hands. Exhale and bend your left knee. Your thigh should be parallel to the floor and your knee should be above the ankle. Hold the pose for several seconds, then straighten your legs. Turn your left foot in and the right foot out and repeat the pose to the other side.

Triangle (Trikonasana) is a pose aimed at mobilizing the hips and stretching the torso. It should also open your chest to allow you to breathe deeply. Begin by standing on Mountain Pose. Step your feet wide apart. Make sure that your hips are facing to the front and lengthen your body, opening up the front of your hips. Turn your right leg, including your thigh, knee and foot, out by 90 degrees. Turn your left leg in about 15 degrees. Raise your arms to shoulder level with your palms facing down towards the floor. Inhale and extend your spine and body upwards and out through the fingertips.

On an exhale, stretch your upper body to the right. Your right hip should still be on the same plane as your shoulders. Place your right hand on your right shin, as far down as you can reach comfortably. If you are more flexible, place your hand on the ground behind your calf. Make sure that your chest is open and your spine is straight. Lengthen your ribs and lift from the edge of your left hip. Raise your left arm towards the ceiling, with your palm facing forward. Gaze at your outstretched hand. Open the chest and turning your belly button slightly upwards. You should feel a twist from your left hip up through the spine. Breathe, increasing the twist on each exhalation. Inhale and allow your body to come to standing.

Repeat the pose on the other side.

BALANCE POSE

Tree (Vrksasana) is a pose aimed to perfect the balance and focus of the mind. In this pose, the lower body provides the support for the upper body as the body stands with grace and strength.

Stand in Mountain Pose. Shift your weight gradually from your left foot to your right foot and focus your awareness on your feet. With your eyes open, fix your gaze on a point a few feet away from you. It's important to pick a point that is not moving, since gazing at this fixed spot with help you find balance and support you from falling. Shifting your weight slowly onto you right leg, keep it strong as you bring your heel into your right ankle. Left toe is pointed on the floor. If you feel safe and comfortable begin to raise your left resting either on your calf with your knee turned outward or on your inner thigh. Make sure your toes are pointing to the floor.

You can use your hand to guide your foot if you want. Using your left hand, gently draw your left knee back to help open up your hip. As you perform this step, be conscious of the position of your hips; they should be squared and facing directly in front of you. Lengthen your spine by pointing your tailbone towards the floor and drawing in the pelvic bone. Pull your bellybutton towards your spine and extend your spine by lowering your shoulders as you lengthen the back of your neck.

Bring your hands towards your chest and press your palms together. On an inhale, if you are balanced, raise your arms above your head. Open up your chest by squeezing your shoulder blades together. Keep easing your bent knee backward. Keep your gaze fixed and remember to breathe easily. Hold the pose for 3 breathes. Lower your arms slowly. Rotate your left leg in front of you so that your bent knee points ahead of you. Straighten your bent leg by raising your foot in front of you and then slowly lowering it to the floor.

Repeat to the other side.

Now move to the floor for bending and relaxation poses.

BENDING POSES

Cat Pose (Bidalasana) is a pose that helps increase flexibility in your spine. When practiced regularly, this pose can help alleviate back pain. It also stretches your neck and helps to stimulate your abdominal organs.

Get on your hands and knees on the floor. Keep your hands directly beneath your shoulders and your knees directly beneath your hips. Breathe in deeply. On an exhale, gently pull your abdominal muscles backwards and towards your spine. Tuck your tailbone down and under. Gently contract your glutes (bums). Spread your fingers. Your middle finger should be facing forward. Gaze at the floor. Press the middle of your back towards the ceiling. Your spine should be rounded upwards. Curl your head inwards. Look at the floor between your knees. Don't force your chin to your chest. Repeat 10 to 20 times. Release by sitting backwards on your heels with your torso upright.

Seated Forward Bend (Paschimothanasana) is a pose that stretches your neck, back, hamstrings, and calves. It also helps alleviate stress. Sit down on the floor with your legs stretched straight out in front of you. Point your toes towards the ceiling. Stretch your lower back and raise your arms above your head. Look forward. Slowly bend forward. Stretch the crown of your head upwards. Try not to let your lower back cave in; you should be bending at your hips. Don't let your legs move or tilt. Stop when you can't bend further without moving your lower back. Place your hands on your lower legs, ankles, or feet. Lightly pull on them to continue stretching with each exhale. Stretch your arms out forward. Hold for a moment. Then, slowly raise your torso up. Try not to move your legs. Sit up straight. Keep your arms above your head as if they were at the beginning of the pose.

Child (Balasana) is a forward bend as well as a resting or restorative pose. You can perform the child's pose to stretch out your lower back between back bends or as a place to recover during a any practice. Kneel on the floor with your legs together and sit back on your heels. Let your arms hang at your sides. Hinge forward until your chest rests on your thighs and your forehead on the floor. If you need to, you can use your hands to guide yourself forward. Curl your shoulders forward and let your hands extend out stretching through the shoulders. You may also let your hands rest palm up next to your feet. Relax into the pose for five breaths.

151

MEDITATIVE AND RESTING POSTURE

Corpse Pose (Savasna)—Call it "rest" pose versus "corpse" for the girls as it is a resting pose. It is typically done at the end of the class as final relaxation. This pose allows the body time to process information at the end of a class. Even though Savasana is a resting pose, it's not the same a sleeping! You should stay present and aware during the five to ten minute duration of final relaxation.

Have the girls lie on their backs. Let the feet fall out to either side. Bring the arms alongside the body, but slightly separated from the body, and turn the palms to face upwards. Relax the whole body, including the face. Let the body feel heavy. Let the breath occur naturally. To come out, first begin to the deepen the breath. Then move the fingers and toes, awakening the body. Bring the knees into the chest and roll over to one side, keep the eyes closed. Slowly bring yourself back up into a sitting position.

~

End with "Namaste." Tell the girls to honor the light within themselves. Let it shine bright often and to have an awareness of how their body appreciates different styles of exercise.

PART 5: HAND OUTS AND WRAP UP

<u>Under the Pillow Affirmation Handout:</u> Each girl in the class will receive an envelope with a special message on the front and a few "positive affirmation" cards inside. These will be unique and specific to each girl. The instructor will be given several messages to choose from. The instructor will include 4-5 cards per girl based on what they feel is most important to communicate to the girl. An example of a finished envelope is attached.

Thoughts to take with you:

Inside this envelope are things that I know to be true about you. Tuck them under your pillow and read them every night before bed and then again in the morning. They will remind you that YOU have the power to be amazing every day!

I write a hand-written note on each envelope to each girl, with things that I believe to be true. Some of my shyest girls emerge throughout the program and I tell them, "You are an amazing leader," because those are things they probably haven't heard about themselves and they would probably not ever describe themselves that way. But it's important for them to know that I see that in them. We tell the girls to keep the envelopes with the cards under their pillows. I want them to read the affirmations inside every night before their heads hit the pillow and every morning before their feet hit the floor! A lot of moms love this activity. They'll say, "Oh my gosh, that's such a great activity!" Or, "My daughter loves to read her cards every night before bed and every morning!"

Dear (Name),

Thoughts to take with you:

Inside this envelope are things that I know to be true about you. Tuck them under your pillow and read them every night before bed and then again in the morning. They will remind you that YOU have the power to be amazing every day!

(Instructor Name)

Class Commencement: Have the girls come back together in a group. Give them some positive feedback from the class. Remind them to get enough sleep so that they keep themselves feeling fabulous and energized.

Hand out the Positive Affirmation Cards to each girl and ask that they wait to open them until they get home. Let them know that each of them is special and the messages inside are just for them. Remind them to read their cards every night before falling asleep and then again when they wake up.

Verbally Assign Homework: Encourage the girls to remember to do something relaxing each night before bed. It can be reading, drawing, reading their cards or whatever they find that helps them wind down from their day. They should also track their sleep patterns this week with the feeling faces worksheet/handout.

Greet Parents: Greet the parents as they come for pick-up and answer any questions they have. Positive energy and friendliness go a long way!

EQUIPMENT AND MATERIALS

If mats or blocks are available to you in the room use them. Otherwise, no *equipment* at this time. The following are materials needed:

- Feeling Faces Worksheet
- Fabric markers
- Pillow case, bookmarks and stickers or T-shirts, depending on what activity you select

Positive Affirmation Cards should be put together in advance and ready to hand out at the end of this class. To put them together you will need:

- Envelopes
- Card stock used to print letter

- Glue stick to glue letter to outside of envelope
- Preprinted positive affirmation cards

SLEEP PATTERN WORKSHEET

(Also known as the "Feeling Faces Worksheet")

Night	Lights Out	Wake Up	Feeling (Happy/Sad/Other)
Monday	___:___ p.m.	___:___ a.m.	🙂 🙁 ◯
Tuesday	___:___ p.m.	___:___ a.m.	🙂 🙁 ◯
Wednesday	___:___ p.m.	___:___ a.m.	🙂 🙁 ◯
Thursday	___:___ p.m.	___:___ a.m.	🙂 🙁 ◯
Friday	___:___ p.m.	___:___ a.m.	🙂 🙁 ◯
Saturday	___:___ p.m.	___:___ a.m.	🙂 🙁 ◯
Sunday	___:___ p.m.	___:___ a.m.	🙂 🙁 ◯

POSITIVE THOUGHTS

FOR THE WEEK AND BEYOND!

If you continue to tell yourself you are amazing then you will be!

We ARE what we think!

YOU have the POWER, GIRL!

Rest is as important to your body as healthy food and exercise.

BACKGROUND AND THEORY

FOOD AND SLEEP

A CHILD'S DIET is a huge factor in their ability to sleep well. I am often a little surprised at what many parents don't know. I guess I have taken for granted what we are aware of and how we eat and sleep in my own house. After all, it's what I do, study health and nutrition as well as sleep. It's what I love, but if that's not someone's background or what they love, how would people know? We live in a society where people are fooled all the time, between all of the false and misleading labeling (such as "all natural ingredients") and the billions spent on advertising for processed foods.

And for the class on sleep we do something special, we end with a short list of positive thoughts while we do yoga. Right when the girls are in relaxation laying down, often giggling, I tell them to relax, and to close their eyes. I'll help them along by telling them to ground themselves to the earth, that their eyes feel heavy, and that they should focus on their breath. I then instruct them to repeat some love and kindness meditation that I have created for them. For example, "I am safe." They then say to themselves, "I am safe."

We continue in this way with other sayings like, "I feel joy, I am beautiful, I am peaceful, I am kind." And I might customize the sayings based on the class or based on the girls. It's so important that they repeat these things to themselves. It's empowering and it allows me to teach the girls about self-love and care. I find parents love this part of the program for their girls. They love that I'm teaching them relaxation techniques but they also love that I'm telling them to go to bed! I tell the girls, "When your parents tell you it's time to go to bed, don't give them any lip! Don't give them a hassle because it's very important that kids get their rest."

I explain to the girls all the important things our bodies are doing when we're sleeping. You are recharging your batteries, your brain is developing, your body—muscles, organs, bones and everything that makes you "you"—is growing. That's hard work and requires rest! Kids can't run on empty, and sleep-deprived kids don't function as well as well-rested kids. I explain that sleep plays a huge roll in a child's development. I teach the girls that if they are sleep-deprived they won't be able to focus, their metabolism won't work as efficiently, and their energy will be zapped. Their studies might suffer and they won't be able to enjoy all the things they might love, like playing sports or running around with friends.

So it's really important for kids to get the proper amount of rest, and the proper amount is actually much more than most people think. Most kids are not getting enough sleep on a daily basis. Kids, all the way through their teenage years, need more sleep than adults because their bodies are so hard at work developing. So how much sleep is enough? When I teach this class to girls and share proper rest recommendations with their parents they are often both shocked. Children Ages 7 to 12 require 10-11 hours of sleep per day. Girls 12-18 should be getting 8 to 9 hours of sleep per night. In most cases kids are not getting enough sleep.

This whole Girl Power program and book are about creating and nurturing healthy, strong girls and this part about sufficient sleep is a huge component in the overall well being of a child. My work is to help both girls and their parents or caregivers understand the importance of rest at every stage of life. Girls need to create good sleeping habits as soon as possible. Parents and kids need to work together to establish a healthy bedtime routine. The routine should be the same or similar every evening. How do girls settle down for bedtime? Reading is a great way to settle down for bed, or perhaps taking a shower or a bath before getting tucked in works best for you. Bedtime meditation can be a powerful tool for children that struggle with a bedtime routine.

Sometimes with the girls I have them track their sleep. For a week I have them track what time they go to bed, what time they wake up and then how they felt. And sometimes they come back if they didn't get a lot of rest and we talk about it: "Oh, I see you felt grumpy. Maybe you got five hours of sleep and you really need nine hours."

Whatever is relaxing and does not involve electronics or television works. Quiet time is important as girls transition from their busy days into bed for a restful night of sleep. Proper rest in children is an absolute must for a healthy, active, balanced life. Kids *must* get their rest in order to feel and perform at their best!

I teach girls to look at sleep in a positive mindset. It's a gift and they all deserve that gift of rest!

CLASS #8: REVIEW AND GRADUATION

IN THIS CHAPTER

CLASS ORGANIZATION AND MATERIALS

PART 1: KICK OFF YOUR FINAL CLASS

<u>Get the Group Moving:</u> Have the group spread out and warm up with dynamic stretching, jumping jacks, running in place or laps around the room, then static stretching. Do this for 3-5 minutes to warm up and help them burn some excited energy. Then call the group to sit in front of you.

<u>Gather all the girls:</u> Review last week's homework as well as previous classes. Talk with the girls about what they liked most about their classes and what they will take with them beyond the classroom. Let them share their thoughts and feelings about the classes. What was their favorite class and why? What fitness activity did they like the most? Was it kickboxing, yoga, boot camp style, or the plyometric work?

PART 2: ACTIVITY

<u>Paper and Self Portrait Activity:</u> Hand out the self-portrait sheet to each girl. Have them spread out on the floor and create. Be sure to have your folder with the portraits from the first class so that you can make comparisons from that first portrait to graduation. What is different? Did anyone draw herself very small in week one and very large in the last portrait? Compare any backgrounds or added features in the

picture. Was the first portrait done with a straight smile and this portrait done with a big smile?

Let the girls share their pictures with the rest of the group if they would like. Bring the portraits out from the first week and compare them. If you see ones with significant changes take pictures of them. The girls may take them home or leave them with you, whatever they would like. If you take pictures please be sure to send them to me at the end of class.

Have them all help pick up the supplies as they are finished.

PART 3: FREESTYLE FITNESS

<u>Mini Boot Camp:</u> Set up a mini boot camp consisting of a few different exercise stations for the girls to go through. Set up

- One station with jump ropes,
- One with a cone zigzag course, and
- One with hula hoops.

Let them choose what station they would like to use. Let the girls enjoy 5 to 10 minutes of "freestyle fitness," meaning they can do whatever activity they would like.

Do some kickboxing, running drills, or plyometric work if you have time at the end of class.

Have the girls do "I am Statements" while they are at stations and exercising. Let them give you words and do many of them! This class is a celebration of what they have learned and how they view themselves—strong, smart, amazing!

Clean Up: Have the group help pick up all the equipment

PART 4: GRADUATION AND WRAP UP

Class Commencement: Have the girls come back together in a group. Give them some positive feedback from the class. Review all that they have learned and how far they have come. Express what the experience gave you and read the graduation letter to all the girls. Be sure you sign all the letters and give one to each girl. Read the graduation certificate to the girls and hand them out to each with the graduation gift. The gift will be a Girl Power water bottle, Girl Power Cinch bag or Girl Power t-shirt. Be sure to sign the graduation certificates and letters in advance.

Greet Parents: Greet the parents as they come for pick-up and answer any questions they have. Wish all the girls and their families well until you see them again. Positive energy and friendliness go a long way! Remind them to be fabulous!

EQUIPMENT AND MATERIALS

- Jump ropes
- Hula hoops
- Flat, round cones
- Radio and music
- Self-portrait blank pages
- Bin of markers and colored pencils
- Graduation certificates (signed)
- Graduation gift (Girl Power water bottles, Girl Power cinch bags or a Girl Power t-shirts)
- Graduation letter with final positive thoughts (signed)

SELF-PORTRAIT BLANK SHEET

Name:_____ Date:_____

Draw a picture of yourself ☺

POSITIVE THOUGHTS

FOR THE WEEK AND BEYOND!

You are AMAZING just the way you are!

Your body will do ANYTHING you set your mind to!

Think it, Believe it, Achieve it!

Do ONE thing every day that makes you HAPPY!

You have ONE body, take care
of it.

We ARE what we think.

Know that your body is
changing but it is just as it
should be right now! Love
every stage!

Nothing worth having is
achieved without hard work
and determination.

GRADUATION CERTIFICATE SAMPLE

I have a graduation certificate for each girl stating that they've successfully completed this eight-week course of Girl Power along with some of the key things they've learned. I've included a sample on the next page, and a blank certificate is provided in the *Girl Power Journal.*

Girl Power

Certificate of Graduation

has successfully completed the 8-week Girl Power Program
offered by Girl Power Go, LLC.

Take all that you have learned
and be the BEST you that you can be!
Think it – Believe it – Achieve it
You have the POWER to do great things!

Approved by
Erin C. Murray
Creator of Girl Power

_____   _____/_____/_____
Signature of Instructor   Date

173

BACKGROUND AND THEORY

GIRLS LOVE THIS CLASS

THE GIRLS LOVE THIS CLASS and although it's a celebration it's also sometimes sad. The eight-week program always goes by too fast for both me and the girls and we never want it to end! For the last class, the eighth class that includes a review of the program and a graduation celebration, I wanted to do something very special for all the girls. I wanted to point out to them that over these last eight weeks they've learned so much about themselves and others. But perhaps the most important thing I want to leave with them is that they are *all* extremely important to *me*. I think in the end a huge part of empowering girls is making them feel strong, smart, powerful, and valuable. I know that it's my best work to help girls realize that they have real value and impact in the world.

My approach is about loving, educating, and supporting the *whole person*! For that reason this program touches on all of those things. We always have a class topic, we do an activity that relates to the topic and then we do physical activities that relate to the week's topic. The girls "get it" and this process works! We talk about lots of things throughout the eight-week course and at graduation we talk about what their favorite things were. In the beginning we asked, "What do you think Girl Power is going to be like," or I might ask them "What have you heard about Girl Power?" At graduation I ask, "What did you love? Was it better than you thought? What class was your least favorite? It's okay if there's a class you really didn't like." Up until the very last moment of the very last class the girls are learning about themselves and each other!

SELF PORTRAITS

Before and after self-portraits, from Class #1 and Class #8

So in Class #8 we begin with a warm up, as usual, and we then discuss their favorite things from the entire course, as above. Then the girls do a new self-portrait. They've now done a new self-portrait in Class #8 as well as in Class #1. I bring out the self-portraits from Class #1. We compare the two. I don't go too deep into analyzing the portraits with the girls, especially the younger girls, because I want that to be something that continues to develop. Sometimes they'll say to me, "Mrs. Mahoney, look! Isn't it funny that I drew myself so small and now look how big my head is!"

"Oh wow, that's so crazy, I love it!" I'll say. "You know, I like that second portrait better," or something like that. I keep it Simple and know in my heart that this program works to empower girls! It's proven and I get to see the proof over and over again. It happens in every town I teach in, every school, every group of girls. In that moment my heart could break right open! Overjoyed doesn't even begin to describe the feeling and the warmth in my heart. It's in that very clear moment that I know the work that I'm doing matters. It has impact and it is changing the path for many girls.

Before and after self portraits

I have had many moms come into the class and look at the portraits with me. If they know about self portraits they might have said things to me like, "Oh my gosh, this is the proof in the pudding that she feels like she has a bigger presence now!" One mother told me that she knew just from her daughter participating in these activities, from talking through our scenarios in class and learning about positive thinking and life lessons in Girl Power, that she was happier and more confident.

Self-portraits speak volumes to one's self esteem, self-worth, and self-love. When a girl draws herself larger, brighter, happier, and standing on her own in the second self-portrait that she creates at the end of the eight-week program we have visual proof that she feels bigger, brighter, stronger, more confident, and empowered!

PARTING POSITIVE THOUGHTS

Then, after some fitness, we do our final and most special "I Am" statements, positive thoughts they can take with them, some of the ones I feel are most important, such as:

"Do one thing every day that makes you happy!"

"Be brave and courageous!"

"Be kind and caring!"

"Know that you have the POWER to impact others in a positive way!"

"You have one body, take care of it!"

"Your body is changing, but it is just as it should be right now. Love every stage!"

GIRL POWER GIFTS

We clean up and we're ready to wrap up the program. I make sure they get something to take with them that represents the program, whether it's a Girl Power t-shirt or a Girl Power water bottle, Girl Power headband, whatever. One time I had a girl donate a bunch of bracelets, and it was funny because I think I gave them out like two years ago, and there was a girl at one of my son's hockey games recently, and her mom pointed out to me that she still wears that bracelet every day. It was really special.

MY LETTER TO THE GIRLS

But way more important than the material gift I give them is telling them how I feel. We review the "most important things" that have come out of these last eight weeks together. They are the things that my mother would say, "you can't buy." I wrote the girls a letter and I tell them how they have impacted me and the power that they have to impact others.

They now have the tools to care for themselves and others in a very positive way. I wrote the letter that follows to the girls when I did this the first time almost seven years ago. It came from my heart and it's part of the package for the last class. Here's a copy of the letter I wrote for them:

To my Girl Power Girls,

Continue to do the work that you have begun here. You are perfect just as you are. I am forever changed because I have had the pleasure of working with you. I hope that you have enjoyed this experience, even half as much as I have. Go after whatever you want in this life, I believe you will achieve great things.

Be Strong! Be Smart! Be Amazing!

With Love and Care, Mrs. Mahoney

SENDING THEM OFF

Girls will feel better after doing this program. They will make better decisions, they will think about their actions before they take them. They will be kind and loving to others and take responsibility when they make a mistake. They will love themselves more along the way and see their own beautiful value and talents. My hope is that they will analyze and dwell on their weaknesses and fears less and move through life the best that they can, knowing that their best is always good enough. As I tell them every week and at every opportunity, "Your best is always good enough because your best is your best!"

I do my best to send them off in a way that says be brave and courageous, to do the right thing when no one else does even if it doesn't make you popular. Take care of YOU, take care of each other, and be strong and kind. We do the "I Am" statements and I always say to them, "Yes you are, and don't let anyone tell you different." We do that from the very beginning and to the very end because I know its deep value. The girls benefit greatly from hearing that over and over. It empowers them to say it and helps them to believe it!

Some girls are sad to see the eight weeks end, and yes, Mrs. Mahoney is always a little sad, too. Sometimes we shed tears. But I always include some giggles and then I send them off with the hopes that they will live their GIRL POWER!

The Future of Girl Power

Organic Development

WHEN I LOOK at this program that I've created called Girl Power it brings me back. I started with the Brownies and the Girl Scouts. Coming from my background in fitness and nutrition that was an obvious starting point. But this was an empowerment program. "The Power of You" was really my first class. I thought, what did my niece Gaby need when she had that problem with this other little girl? She needed to feel like she could stand up for herself. And I wanted her to be, frankly, like a bad-ass. I wanted her to stand in her power, but I wanted her to do it in a way that was kind and caring and loving, so she could feel proud of herself, and in a way that no mom was going to call us and say, "Oh my gosh—Gaby was mean to my daughter!"

It was kind of, "How can I teach girls to rise above the noise? How can I teach girls to stand up for themselves while still being loving and kind? there is so much "noise" out there for kids and grown-ups. So how can we just quiet the noise and stand up with power and say, "This is what I'm feeling. I can handle this and look back at this and feel really proud of myself"? So I think that was the start of the first part of Girl Power. Then as I got to know these girls and their parents and with teaching more it all seemed to fall into place over time to become the program it is today.

For example, people have come to me over the years and said things to me like, "I have this Girl Scout troop and they're fourth graders and they're really struggling. This is a place where girls really struggle with friends."

"Oh, sure," I'd say, "I'll create a class for that!" unafraid.

I felt like I knew I had the knowledge because I was a girl who struggled with friendships with other girls, who at times questioned my self-confidence and didn't always make the right decisions. I felt I had something to contribute because of my career background coupled with my life journey thus far. I felt comfortable and confident with all of that and I love working with kids so all of those components came together, and as I developed classes I started to see, "Wow, this issue or topic is bigger than this one class and even this one group. I know every group of girls could benefit from this. I know thousands of girls must be struggling with the same things."

So I think that it's a mix between what the need was at the time and what I felt was important—obviously "Love and Kindness," for one example. I thought good friends and loving kindness are very similar, even the activities can be similar, but they are different topics. One without the other isn't enough. So we talk about it the next week, after we come back from navigating relationships and being a good friend, we need to come back and have the reminder of the love and kindness. I felt like I wanted to carry that through the entire program. First we talk about it with friends, and that's a big step, that girls can be brave and courageous (which is from the Warrior Class).

They all kind of go together but they are just additional pieces. One builds on the other. They can stand well on their own, if I have a group that is looking for something specific, but as far as an eight-week program for this book or the workbook, it's so important for them to do all of the pieces.

Kids, adults, everybody learns in different ways so maybe it's the physical exercises where a girl connects or an activity that we're doing; maybe it's the lesson plan part where we sit on the floor and we talk through their situations. At some point I'm hoping to scoop up all of the girls. Maybe they get a little piece in the Good Friends class, then they pick up more when we talk through the Love and Kindness. Then the healthy eating, and that goes right into the Sleep class. All of those things are important, so it's really to nourish the whole child—their minds, their thoughts, their physical being, how they take care of themselves, that's all part of it. If we leave out any part, then we're kind of missing the boat.

It has evolved and grown in a very organic way. I could have gone on forever, and I still do. For example, I mention there is a class that is kind of a spin-off from the Good Friends class. I call it The Problem with Three. And that could be an adult class or a kid class. Sometimes I'll have a Girl Scout class that needs a little bit more. Maybe in the third grade they do Good Friends with me and then maybe in the fifth grade before they go to middle school they need a little more, maybe The Problem with Three, and navigating a little bit deeper into these relationships. That one isn't part of the eight weeks but it's still very important and very real. It just depends on what people's needs are.

Sometimes when you're so focused on what you're doing, it takes someone else to point out your progress. As I said, I like to give them some kind of gift at that last class. One of the first things I did with one of my bigger classes was I got these kind of burlap bags from a craft store. I got some iron-on logo paper. I remember ironing them and cutting them— my gosh, I had that ironing board out for days. My son Jack looked at me like I was crazy and asked me, "What are you doing?"

"Someday," I said, "these are going to be flying off a press in some warehouse."

We laughed about it then. Jack came with me when I took the ride about two years later to get my first box of t-shirts. As we stood in the warehouse and talked to the guys that worked the machinery and mixed the colors, we got to see how the shirts were made. When we got back into the car my son Jack said to me, "Mom, you told me that someday the Girl Power logo thing would be coming off the press somewhere, and look—it is!"

We both laughed and I think we knew it was only the beginning! That was many years ago now, that Jack remembers me cutting and ironing all night in our living room, and maybe three years ago that we had our first big batch of t-shirts created, and the ride has been non-stop fun and excitement ever since.

SEMINARS AND WORKSHOPS

SO WHAT DOES the future hold? Well in addition to making Girl Power available everywhere by publishing books, as both a program for schools and groups—and with these books Girl Power also becomes something a mom or dad can do with their daughter(s) at home—there are also seminars and workshops you might consider attending, organizing, or even leading. My friend Gina is a Girl Scout leader who is a real go-getter. She heard about me and reached out to me, and we've done some really big events together by now, some with over 60 girls, and at least one event with over 100 girls. So in that situation we talk about the age group of the girls and what we want to do, and then I pick some classes from the eight-weeks, and I tailor them to the time frame. Let's say we did a two-hour class or workshop. We get all the girls registered and Gina and I work together. Girl Scout girls who do two classes with me get a Girl Power "fun patch." In workshops it's really fun for me. I have patches that say Girl Power and Girl Power Go and in Brownies and Girl Scouts it's a big deal. Everybody loves a fun patch, including me!

So my curriculum syncs up with three of their different badges, depending on what journey they're on and what stage they're at. There is one that's called "My Best Self," and there is one for healthy snacking and "Your Best Year," is another one. My classes meet the requirements for girls to earn those patches.

Gina has helped me do some of those big workshops and Girl Power events. When I began doing these larger events and helping girls feel empowered, prepare for middle school, and deal with friends, the word traveled fast. Soon I had Girl

Scout leaders from other towns coming to observe and see what this "Girl Power thing" was all about. They helped me to bring it to their towns and this happened over and over. Once people saw me and this program in action it was just a matter of finding the space and date to teach.

The Preparing for Middle School workshop I have created is one of my favorites to do on a large scale. There are towns with four or five elementary schools and they all funnel into the same middle school. A lot of these girls are nervous. So in the spring, they did a workshop with me and it was all about middle school. We talk about their fears and excitement and I help them to connect to each other. I actually march in there and try to break up any clicks or established groups right away. I get them uncomfortable quick but then spend the next two hours or so helping them to realize that they all share the same fears and excitements, more or less. They also discover how fun and easy it can be to meet and connect with new girls.

It's easy for me to see which girls go to what school and who knows who. When I put the girls into working groups it's important to mix things up. Instead of counting them off, "one, two," and so on, I put them in groups by birth month. Now with Girl Scouts they are usually there because they choose to be but with some of the middle school girls they are there because their mom or dad made them attend my Girl Power class. I ask the girls, "Who is here because you wanted to take this class?" Many times not too many hands go up. Then I ask, "Who is here because Mom or Dad made you come?" Lots of hands go up. I immediately tell them that, "It's okay. You don't want to like this class or maybe even me, but you will. It's okay. We will be on the same page in no time!" And I kind of just put it right out there. I think the girls like and respect that I don't hold back and I'm just being me. I tell them that I too had fears and excitement about middle school and it's completely natural. This is their opportunity to work through all of it before they arrive at middle school in the fall.

We proceed to do activities together as a group. They even have to do a presentation. One, for example, with the middle school group, had to do with "Everything is changing on the inside and out!. Your body is changing, your friends are changing, your locker, your school, your teachers, maybe your bus routine is changing." In this workshop I love to tell them, "Your best friend might be right here and you haven't even met her yet. Look around. I know you're really comfortable with the friends you had in elementary school, but middle school is an awesome place." I'll tell them, "There's excitement and then there's fear. What gets your heart pumping more than those two things? You're super-excited to go to this big place that we don't know anything about, but man, it really seems kind of scary."

And then I talk to them a little bit about fear. I believe fear is not real, it's made up, and it's in our heads. So I love to talk about conquering our fear. I like to say "Be fearless!" Girls love that. We talk about those things and they end up doing a big project. We also talk about how we need to take care of ourselves, to take care of each other, our friends and our families. How do you help and serve others as well as your school and your community? We talk about recycling, for example. We talk about how they are evolving in a very exciting way, and that they can become the best version of themselves in this place we call middle school.

These are cool examples of bigger workshops that I do and I want to move more towards that because I feel like we can touch more girls' lives that way. That's my vision for after this book comes out—I'd like to do bigger workshops and events. I love to see the impact that these events have had on girls. I know I'm giving them the tools they need to make the most of the next phase of their lives. I help them to create a positive daily practice of positive affirmations and self-love activities, reminding them to always do their best and that their best is always good enough. After all, your best is your best, right? Yes, that's right!

I work with local leaders and teachers and discuss what the hot topics are at the moment and how Girl Power can bring the most value to their school or organization. Sometimes it's a "Good Friends" or a "Love and Kindness" event but many times we like to start with "The Power of You" class or event. It gets girls introduced to Girl Power and sets the stage for positive impact in the future. It all starts with reminding girls that they have choices—big, exciting choices about who they want to be and how they want to live their lives. Many times my classes or events are the first time they have heard this and it's so true. I tell them, "Your life is happening right now so choose to live it in the best way that you can, a way that makes you feel good inside!

GIRL SCOUTS

I ALSO DO A LOT of work with Girl Scouts of America. This is very in-line with them. I'm what they call a Community Partner with Girl Scouts in Massachusetts. They hire me to come in and teach my Healthy Living Class, or

The Importance of Rest, or I have a class that's called Brave and Courageous and I actually paint the girls' faces with face-painting crayons. We talk about being brave and courageous, about doing the right thing when no one else does, and those kind of things, and then I turn them into warriors and we kickbox. We talk about standing in that on-guard stance, but we also talk about being open to change and relationships and new situations, and about being really strong. They hire me for individual classes but I think, *Gosh, there could be a whole manual for Girl Scout leaders.* They could get the manual and the supplies and know this is how you teach it. I'd love to see Girl Power fully implemented by the Girl Scouts in the near future, and I believe it will be.

MY WILDEST HOPE

BUT MY WILDEST HOPE is that I have thousands of girls going to bed at night with these empowerment books, the *Girl Power Guidebook* and companion *Girl Power Journal*, making them feel really good about themselves. I hope they can relate to a character in the book or the positive affirmations or the "I Am" statements. I hope they might relate to some of the stories that I have shared from when I was younger or from the lessons I have created and shared to help them navigate through with love, kindness, and peace. I hope that they practice saying good things to themselves daily, whether it's at the end of every chapter, activity, or lesson. I want each girl reading these books to be engaged and also feel like a little powerhouse, like "Man, I can do anything! I'm going to tackle my day. I know that I can because I'm reading this great Girl Power empowerment book and following along in the journal and it makes me feel strong, smart, positive, healthy and empowered."

I feel so happy that I've created Girl Power and that it does make girls see that they can do these exercises, and that it's giving them the tools that they need to feel really good about themselves. I love that it has the potential to help parents with their daughters or grandparents with their grand-daughters. So maybe because of this program and these books girls will be better armed or equipped when someone says something not so nice to them, or when someone says something outright mean! Maybe they'll help someone that's feeling uncomfortable, or unsafe or insecure. I tell them, "Be that girl that cares and does the right thing. Be a brave leader and others will follow. Be that girl that would stand beside you in any situation and always have your back."

And my vision is to get Girl Power out to the world. I'd love to translate these books into every language. Crazy-brilliant Sean Roach gave me that idea. I told him I wanted to bring Girl Power nationwide and he said, "You are a small thinker!" I almost fell over—we were in 18 towns at the time and I had four instructors on and off working for or with me. All of this from me and my mouth! Spreading the word about Girl Power one person, adult, school, child, friend or colleague at a time. What Sean said to me next blew my mind and changed my world! Sean said, "You should write a book, translate it into every language and go global!" *Seriously? Is this guy for real?* I thought, then I jumped in with both feet. I knew in that moment that *I have to work with this person and his team!* And here we are! As scary and uncertain as it's been I have not one single regret. I am supposed to bring this program and these lessons to the world!

And I'm hoping that after reading this book, you too have the idea that you would love to work with Girl Power and Girl Power Go. Girls need this program and these books, today more than ever, and it works—it works as much as you put your love and passion into it! Time is proving that the lessons the girls learn in Girl Power they take with them. The power of this program is that girls carry on a "Girl Power" way of living and behaving. They hold onto the lessons and activities, they do them over and over. They practice kindness and care and when they make mistakes they take responsibility. They are able to implement and learn again and again how to handle so many things that are in their paths. They see the value in the program and they are excited to share it with others. If I can empower one girl to love herself more, be kind and patient with another person, extend a helping hand when it's not convenient or when they might rather not, to step out of her comfort zone, to speak and act with love and care, and to take good care of themselves with proper nutrition, sleep, and activity, then I have done really good work!

And that gets me super-excited—how about you?

—ERIN MAHONEY, CREATOR OF GIRL POWER

JANUARY 12, 2017

MILFORD, MASSACHUSETTS

TESTIMONIALS

CONFIDENCE AND FINDING ONE'S VOICE

by MARGIE WIGGIN

WHEN I MET ERIN I was working at the Elmwood School in Hopkinton, which is a grade 2 and 3 elementary school. Her niece, Gaby, was at my school and the same age as my daughter Molly. They were both also in my Girl Scout troop—I was a Girl Scout leader for them. I met Erin through moms and daughters in Girl Scouts. I also knew of Erin's son, Jack, who would come to school in a Spiderman outfit, the one with the built-in muscles. He would come through the door and he would do that little jump and say, "Spidermaaaaan!" He was just the cutest little guy! So I knew Jack—I knew Spiderman—and I knew Erin, and I knew Gaby, I was her Girl Scout leader. I became very interested in what Erin was doing and we would chat. She told me she was doing this Girl Power thing, starting it out.

Now, I am also a Reiki master, and very interested in energy, and positive thinking, and all of this study comes together for me to help people be all they can be. Erin and I are aligned philosophically, with our outlook on how to live in the world, and how to be a success in the world. We're active, interested, intelligent, women. Erin is using her fabulous energy to channel into this great service and great encouragement to young women to say to them, "Hey, you are powerful too! It's not just Spider-*man*, who is powerful— young women can also be powerful!"

Erin did this wonderful session with the girls at the elementary school, so I said to her, "Hey, I would love if you would do this presentation to my Girl Scout troop." So she came and did this activity they could earn a badge with. I watched her do this and I said, "You know what? I want to take this to the Hopkinton Girl Scout Organization and ask if you could do a presentation at the Bridging[13] ceremony." At the end of year, in town, all the Girl Scouts get together and they advance to their next level—it's a meaningful thing.

---

[13] "Bridging" is when a Girl Scouts moves from one level to the next. It's big deal, a celebration. —E.M.

Well, Erin was able to do a presentation for all the girls that were there for the Bridging ceremony. And from that she has been able to blossom her business, and now everyone is able to see how wonderful she is. It took off like wildfire and a lot of that is because of her energy and conviction in what she's doing. She believes in what she's doing and she puts all of that force behind it. She is her own best advertisement because once you see her in action, you say, "Hey, I want that for my kid! I want that role model, I want that guidance. As my daughter is growing into a woman, I want her to see that she can be powerful," and not in an obnoxious way, but in a strong way, a powerful way.

My daughter, Molly, and Erin's niece, Gaby, are now sophomores in high school, but at the time they were in second or third grade. Molly has many friends, gets good grades, and has been on Principal's Advisory Council, and was asked to go to a conference on bullying as a representative of the school. She has that inclination naturally, but as a result of her going through the Girl Power program Erin only added to her ability to go for it in life. The program really takes a girl to whatever her next level is. My daughter did have some anxiety in life. She definitely feels more powerful now, and I feel the Girl Power program was a contributing factor.

I think Molly was chosen for Principal's Advisory and for the town's Youth Commission because she demonstrated that she is a voice in the community that administrators want to hear from. I think having Molly in Erin's program is part of what supported that voice and helped her be able to feel confident enough to speak up *in a group of adults nonetheless*. I unreservedly recommend Girl Power to any young girl, whether they are dealing with low self-esteem,. anxiety, social awkwardness, or if they are already confident and setting examples for others in their groups. It helps all of them.

"Somebody who has had Girl Power *is* strong."

by Gabrielle, the original Girl Power Girl!

The primary Girl Power superhero is named "Gaby," and modeled after the Gaby you are about to hear from (Illustration by Keith Seidel).

I'M 14 NOW, but when I was seven or eight, there was a girl on my school bus and she would always sit behind me. (I would always sit somewhat towards the front of the bus—not the back because that's where all the older kids were.) She would always end up saying names to me or she would say some really mean things (she called me a tom-boy) and I

199

really didn't know what to do, I was quite confused. It was a first time for me, so I would just kind of let it happen—I really didn't know what to do.

I talked about it with my mom and she told me, "Oh, you've got to stand up for yourself, you have to tell her to back off!" I was really scared because I was really shy back then. I was telling my aunt about it, and she was telling me what to do—all of this stuff totally different from what my mom said, all of these additional ideas.

My aunt Erin found me a shirt that said, *I am not a tom-boy, I'm an athlete,* and I started wearing it on the bus. The older girls didn't know what to do—they left me alone after that. So Aunt Erin had this idea to teach other girls about this, so they wouldn't get into the situation I was, and they would know what to do.

I can remember the first class—it was in my Girl Scout troop, actually. My aunt came to my friend's house and she gave a presentation about what we need to do if girls are picking on us, or boys, or anyone at all. How would we need to deal with it? We called it "Girl Power."

Next, my aunt brought it to my school, Elmwood School in Hopkinton, where I went for elementary school. I remember going to Girl Power classes there. The girl who was picking on me was in the class, so it was kind of awkward. But as I was thinking she was the person who was doing it to me, I realized maybe she's doing it because she's getting picked on as well, or something's happening on her side that is causing her to do this stuff to me.

The Girl Power class was really fun. I can remember I became friends with her—the girl who was picking on me.

We're kind of friends now, we talk a little bit. She has gotten better. She doesn't say anything mean to me anymore.

There was this one drill where we had to give each person a compliment and then give another person a different one. She would always come up to me and say the exact same one: "You look great today!" So in the end it was so much fun and I loved it because now we're good friends. It was really fun.

We came up with new t-shirts. They said "Girl Power" on them, and it was a girl standing, wearing a cape. Whenever I look at it I think, "That's a strong person." I always imagine somebody strong—and somebody who has had Girl Power *is* strong.

Lots of girls at Elmwood, which is a school for second and third graders, did the Girl Power class, and they opened it up to kids of other ages, too, 4th and 5th, and I think some first-graders.

I definitely was shy when I was younger but not anymore. Girl Power is definitely part of why I am not shy anymore. In every Girl Power class we had, Aunt Erin would have us get in front of the class and say something we believe about ourselves. One thing I said was, "I'm a strong person." Hearing myself say that really kind of broke me out of my shell. It made me think what I was saying was true about myself.

I know other girls who went through Girl Power. I have a friend who had a lot of problems with her weight and after she did the program with my aunt she had a different perspective of herself. Now she totally thinks of herself as not being overweight, and not being judged inside other people's heads, like what they think about her isn't important.

201

I'm in high school now, so it's not really a big problem, but in middle school I can remember, I played on the eighth grade soccer team and there were these girls on my team. They would kind of tease me about certain stuff. I didn't really appreciate it, obviously, and no one would stick up for me and I didn't see anybody tell them to back off or anything, so I kind of had to stand up for myself and I confronted them about it, and all I could think about was my aunt in the back of my head telling me, "You can do this! Don't be scared."

I told them, "I don't appreciate you doing what you're doing to me and I need you to stop now."

"Oh, yeah, I didn't know it was bothering you, I'm sorry," they said. It was that easy. Maybe people just need to stand up once in a while.

I definitely think other girls should do Girl Power. I think the best time is about third grade, about the age I was. When girls start early they're carrying it through their lives—like their entire life they're going to use it. It's just a powerful tool.

I'm really proud of my aunt for taking this next step with Girl Power (this book). She's just the best person ever. She's like a second mom to me. If she heard that it would definitely make her cry. Thank you so much! I definitely think other girls should do Girl Power too.

POWERFUL IDEALS

by GINA ARTHUR

WHEN MY GIRL SCOUT TROOP was in fourth grade (they're in seventh now) I attended a Girl Scout workshop for leadership. People share programs they have done and gone to and someone mentioned the Girl Power program to me and it sounded interesting. I wanted to run an event in fourth grade for the Girl Scouts that would bring the local three schools together, because I didn't think our girls were aware that there were other girls in the town that were Girl Scouts as well. So I called Erin and I told her that I wanted to do something to empower girls. I had read a little bit on her website and thought it was the perfect thing to have the girls merge together with, for them to have some fun activities, and to get some positive *girl power* out of it at the same time! Erin ran with it, and it was one of the most successful programs we had done here up to that time, in Natick, Massachusetts.

I now oversee all the Girl Scouts in the area in addition to my own troop, about 500 Girl Scouts. They call me a "Service Unit Coordinator." Basically, I am the liaison between all the troops here and Girl Scouts of Eastern Mass. So when Erin came in and did so great with that first Girl Power program, we opened the program up to the whole town at different levels, every year after her doing it for my own troop.

Girl Power programs would sell out and people were like, "What do you mean, there are no more spaces?"

"I'm sorry—the venue can only take so many spots, you know?" I'd explain.

The program itself was great because she incorporated all of these fun activities like kickboxing, dancing, then they take a little break and write things to empower themselves and about how they feel good about themselves, and I think that's so important with girls. They are taught in the program that they are smart, they're strong, they're amazing—that's the motto, in fact: "Be Strong, Be Smart, Be Amazing,"—but sometimes they don't really believe it even though they know they are supposed to. So Erin does all of these great activities like having the girls write on sticky notes, "I am beautiful," or "I am strong." She tells the girls to put these sticky notes around the house—on a kitchen cabinet, on a vanity mirror, on your locker—so that when you're kind of down in the dumps you see these notes everywhere and cheer up.

My daughter put them all over the house when she did the program, which is really kind of cool. They are still there to this day—and it's been three years! I'll open the cabinet and there's a sticky note in there! Seeing them three years later, I see how they incorporate a lot of that strength and those characteristics Erin had the girls bring out in themselves three years ago. I see those girls now helping the younger kids here in town, doing things with the Brownies or the Daisies, and I'll hear them say some of the very same things Erin was teaching them three years ago. You know, seeing that, that they truly believe these great things and they're kind of showing the younger girls, "You are amazing at this," or "You are great at this," it's so nice to see them mature like that, it's so nice because they're not going to say these things to younger kids if they don't truly believe it themselves.

I've brought Erin back to do the same type of program but at different levels, like the Daisy level, which is kindergarteners and first-graders. We've done the Brownie level, which is second and third graders, and we've done a junior level which is fourth and fifth-graders—because they're just capable of *more* to do at that level. So that was good, breaking up the different levels, because when you have a kindergartener and a fourth-grader, they're in different places.

Ours would ordinarily be a two-hour workshop. All the Girl Scout programs Erin has done I'd say have been about two hours. She would incorporate the kickboxing and an obstacle course in them. She does have a Girl Power patch the girls can get when they do this type of event, which would be a fun event, and which is called a "fun patch." It's really cute—it has the logo on it, "Girl Power Go!" Girl Power and Girl Scouts are good for each other. They are following the same ideals of empowering girls—that they can do anything that they want to.

Often times as the girls get older—more towards fifth, sixth, and seventh grade—these girls who were super motivated and super positive, and who had a lot of self-confidence when they were younger, they can get a little squished when they get into middle school. I don't know why that happens, but I think girls who maybe never believed in themselves to start with but are told to, that they're the ones who tend to have a harder time in middle school. I'm sure hormones and boys and everything else is going haywire at that age. I have had my Girl Scout troop, with 21 girls, since they were five years old, when they were in kindergarten, and I see how much they've matured and grown into these wonderful young ladies. They have self-confidence. I think when we instill that and show them why they are these amazing girls, as they start getting older you can see that they truly believe that in themselves. And when they're then working with the younger girls and trying to do the same things that we did as young adults ourselves—bringing out their own good qualities—you can see them doing this with the younger kids, which is so nice to see. Pretty amazing.

My girls do a lot of community service. They have a great self-image of themselves but they also realize that there are people who need help in the world, and they recognize that they can be that person to help them, whether it be a food pantry or just telling someone that they're great at something. Their language is nice, and I think that when you have programs like Erin's,. it makes them into community leaders. In fact I wish that there were programs like this for boys. I have a son and there's nothing like that out there for the boys, but maybe someday. Boys or girls, when they learn that it's not all about them, they're more aware of others and it's so refreshing because you start to see, "Okay, this next generation, they're going to be okay!"

So Girl Power should absolutely spread beyond the borders of Massachusetts. Troop leaders are always looking for things to do, and the ideals Erin talks about—being a good friend, navigating though relationships, healthy eating, being brave and courageous—all those things are things I know the Girl Scout leaders and any kind of youth leaders of the United States are trying to incorporate into their programming. Sometimes deciding upon and explaining those activities are the hardest parts, so a guidebook and a workbook will be very helpful. The girls love workbooks, they love that stuff even at 13 years old. They compare notes and they share ideas, they love that stuff. And I think the images that they get in their heads from some of the exercises last in their heads. They learn how powerful their words can be, good and not so good! It becomes more real for them. So I would encourage the spread of Girl Power to other programs, absolutely.

WHAT WOULD ERIN DO?

by SHERENE BORR

(This testimonial refers to *another* daughter named "Gabby.")

MY DAUGHTER was in a Girl Scout program and we heard about this "Girl Power" program. A few of the girls signed up and little did I know that one of the mothers in the group had actually gone to high school with Erin. So I knew it was somebody we could trust and that the program was wonderful at that point. Just watching my daughter go through the program and be inspired, feel powerful, feel good about herself was pretty amazing to see. At that time, my daughter was a little shy, so it helped her come out of her shell.

Some of the programs they did were about friendships, how important it is to eat well, to get your sleep, taking care of your body. The one class that my daughter absolutely loved was the Warrior Class (Brave and Courageous). The kids are given face paint and they are encouraged to paint their faces and be warriors. The students then say "I" statements. For example, "I am strong, I am a leader, I'm beautiful." It really empowered the girls. When you think about it we really teach our girls not to be full of themselves, and to always think about other people, but it is important to think about yourself, to think of your body, to think of who you are as a girl in society.

My daughter really loved that class, to put face paint on however you wanted to. It really was a session that brought the girls together. If one girl said, "I am strong," another girl might feel that she too is strong too. And if somebody else said "I am pretty," or "I am beautiful," another girl might think that about herself too, which is really important. It really helps the girls feel empowered and to feel really good about their bodies, which is so important with the stigma of the magazines and the TV shows.

I have talked to my daughter about how the models and the actresses in the magazines are all airbrushed. Their thighs are thinned out, their stomachs and legs are thinned out. My daughter is a dancer and she has really strong legs. I was talking with Erin—and this brought tears to my eyes—and I told her that my daughter Gabby (another "Gabby," different than Erin's niece, "Gaby") said to me, "a lot of the girls have skinnier legs than I do."

"You tell her," Erin said, "that she has strong, powerful legs, and they are beautiful."

That, to me, was so special, because here my daughter feels a little insecure, and Erin sees it as the muscle in my daughter's legs makes her strong, powerful, and beautiful, just the way she's made. This really helped Gabby. And because it came from Erin, Gabby listened—she was okay with it, rather than me as her mother saying, "Gabby, you are beautiful, from head to toe. God made you just the way you are. Everybody is different in their own special way. You were given the strong, powerful, beautiful legs. And you're a dancer, and you're beautiful."

It meant a lot to me, and the class was important for Gabby. Now keep in mind, Gabby did Erin's class back in the second or the third grade and she's in seventh grade now. So for Gabby to take that to heart from Erin now, I'm sure made a real difference for her, and she will remember that for the rest of her life, every time she looks at her legs. And that's important! Because the stereotypes today are that a girl needs to be skinny, you need to be tiny, you need to watch what you eat. Now, we're a pretty healthy family. We do eat snacks but we eat mostly fruit for dessert at night. Once or twice a week we may eat ice cream, but not every night. We also want the kids to enjoy—enjoy their summer, enjoy eating some special snacks—it's okay in moderation.

At the end of the Girl Power class Erin writes a sticky note to each girl and places it in an envelope. The girls are to wait to open them until they get home. Gabby still has hers on her mirror, right where she gets ready, and it says, "You look beautiful." She sees this every morning. I see it when I walk into her room and it brings a smile to my face. My husband sees it. My son sees it. So I guess you could say it helps us all. But for her to still have that little Post-It piece of paper in her room after all these years, it's just wonderful, it really is.

I'm not saying the Girl Power class has helped her with everything, but it has helped her with her health and her body, and to think of herself as a woman. Girls and women have come a long way but we still have a long way to go. Erin has a wonderful class for this in Girl Power. It's a wonderful way for your girl teens, too, to feel empowered, to feel like their goals are important, and to help find their identity.

I just finished my master's degree in educational psychology. I am switching careers to be a school adjustment counselor, so this is right up my alley. I feel honored to be asked for my opinion on Erin's program. I'm so excited about Girl Power I talk about it everywhere I go. When I did my presentation for my graduate class and did it on the subject of Erin's Girl Power program, all the other grad students in my class got excited about having it delivered in their schools as well. It's really important and powerful, and what's so amazing is that you can actually use it in an auditorium with the kids in the school and then break off into smaller groups with the teachers or you can just have the individual sessions with counselors, which is awesome. Girl Power can be delivered to one girl or 400 at a time.

I told Erin whenever she is giving a presentation to a new group I would be happy to speak about my experience with it. I might have my happy tears I get when talking about it with adults, because it's just so beautiful to see how much positive impact one person—Erin in this case—had on my daughter, and to see Girl Power made available to hundreds and even thousands of girls, it's so beautiful to see.

While working on my master's degree, I had a class that required some research and a presentation on a school program of my choice. I interviewed Erin and included her and Girl Power in my presentation. It was awesome because for my presentation Erin gave me a Girl Power t-shirt to wear. And it was so beautiful. I ended my presentation with how Erin was selected as a Hopkinton Hero, which a little girl at that school nominated her for. As I quoted what that little girl wrote in my own presentation to my grad class, I wasn't the only one brought to tears. Three others were as well, including the professor. It was just so beautiful to see the impact on this one girl, who was in the second or third grade. Just to see what she wrote was so amazing.

There are girls who seem confident, but are they really confident? Are they confident because they are trying to act that way, to be more prominent in the society or to be popular? Or are they truly accepting of themselves? Girl Power helps girls become who they really should be. It helps their feelings and it helps them blossom in the world today which is so important. We know today it's tough for young girls with all the social media out there. I'm fearful for my daughter, but confident because she has a core group of four to six really good friends, but it's tough. She has friends she has known since she was two who now don't talk to her when they are with a certain group of people. When she is alone with that friend they are fine. Or when you were invited to sit at a lunch table and it's a set up, when all the other kids get up and leave. That's hard to handle and go through.

My daughter has seen this happen to friends of hers and she helps them now. "Come sit with us, that's no big deal" she tells them. "Real friends would not do that kind of thing."

But it's hard to see my daughter go through that and tear up telling me about it. She and her friends, they are changing. It hurts but it's okay. It's tough but social media makes it ten-times worse. That's why I want to work with both boys and girls in the schools. It's so important because there are so many kids and so many parents in the world who think that kids are perfect. We need to let them know it's okay to make a mistake, because when our kids go off to college and they don't get that or they make a mistake, they're not going to be so hard on themselves that they are going to put themselves down or go into a depression, that they might drop out or even worse.

So I really feel that Erin's classes, that Girl Power will last a lifetime with any girl who goes through the program. It will last with the parents as well, because what goes on are great opportunities for discussions between a parent and a daughter. It's a great time for bonding. Gabby and I did this when she went through Girl Power, and it was so special. She and I don't talk about everything, but she does come to me with a lot of things and it's very nice to have that open communication.

You have the power to make the decisions for yourself, but think about those decisions before you act upon them. Are they helpful? But it also helps in the case of a bully. What do you do? How do you address it? You don't gang up on a bully, of course, but you can tell the bully, "That's not nice! That's not okay!" And Erin goes over all of this in the Girl Power classes.

So my daughter is definitely more confident with herself and I have definitely seen that over the years she has learned to stand up for her friends. One time in about the sixth grade there was a group of kids that came from a foreign country to study at Gabby's school. They were in some of Gabby's classes together as a group. They were sitting by themselves at lunch. So Gabby went out of her way and went over and sat with them, and actually became very good friends with them. Throughout the year they were her besties. Some of the girls have moved but she still stays in touch with them. That was a big deal for her, to leave her friends and sit with the other girls.

She did tell her friends, "Listen, I'm still friends with you, but I want to go sit with these girls for a while and learn from them." Gabby learned about other countries, she teaches them English and they taught her French, Spanish, and Portuguese, and she had a really great year this past year. I think she was empowered through the Girl Power program to go outside of her comfort zone, to go outside of her shell where she normally is.

Gabby has had a few experiences with bullies with her and her friends and she did stand up to them and tell them it's not okay. She did go to the principal and tell him what she knew. It was huge for her to volunteer that information to say, "Mom, I'll go and tell the principal what happened."

So I think my daughter has definitely matured from having done Girl Power. It definitely helps. I wish that I had had something like this. I was definitely an introvert growing up and didn't really come out of my shell until I was about 25 and married my husband. And I try to tell my daughter, "You know, you find out who you really are when you're in your 20's. You're learning now and finding out what you like and what you don't like." And I've definitely seen my daughter blossom this last year, in her maturity, in her feeling confident about herself. Two years ago she got into competitions with her dance and has been just sensational, and I have watched her become a beautiful dancer. To be able to get up on that stage by yourself and do a solo is just so amazing, as well as with all the other girls on stage too. I would not have had the confidence to do that at her age, to get up in front of a full auditorium and dance, and to dance with all her heart.

Gabby will be twelve this year, and it has been four years since she did Erin Mahoney's Girl Power as an eight-week program. In fact it might have been one of the first programs Erin delivered. I love the picture Erin has on her website, with Gabby in it from back then, with all the kids wearing their warrior paint. Gabby was so little then. And it didn't matter how they wore their paint, it was completely up to the kids. They loved it. They got so creative with the paint, some of them even had it on their arms. And even today I try to go back and relate with what can be learned through the Girl Power program. Even today I'll ask her, "Well, what do you think Erin would say?"

HOPKINTON HERO

Erin and Mirabella

EARLY ON IN TEACHING Girl Power at a school in
Hopkinton it came to my attention that the PTA had a
program to honor people in the community who have

impacted a child. The program has the kids writing essays about anyone that they feel has made a difference. So cool, right?! I wasn't even aware of this program until a student nominated me. The program is called "Hopkinton Heroes" and apparently it was a very big deal My sister was a part of the PTA and explained to me that it was a great honor to be nominated by a child. I could see that. I had no idea that one of my Girl Power girls had written and essay about me and our Girl Power work together. The students write hundreds of essays, and they can write about anybody that they have encountered in their school life; a teacher, a janitor, another parent, a cafeteria worker, bus driver—anybody. A girl nominated *me*. So the first time I did a program for the Hopkinton school system for second and third graders, this beautiful girl wrote this essay, *and it got picked!* They then have a reception to celebrate all of the Hopkinton Heroes. We watched a video where the kids read their essays. There were only 13 people honored that year. I cried a lot that night! Tears of joy. Mirabella is the girl that wrote the essay and she was at the reception with me and her parents. It was an amazing evening that I will never forget! To be honored for this work that I do with girls by a child in my classroom. Doesn't get much better than that! Then they frame the child's essay and each Hopkinton Hero gets to take their award home. Mine still hangs with pride in my office. It was crazy to hear "Hopkinton Heroes Congratulates Erin Mahoney"

This is Mirabella's essay:

My Hopkinton Hero is Ms. Erin Mahoney. She's my hero because she tells girls they can make a difference in their lives whenever they want to. She does it by telling girls that they can be strong no matter what. She makes them scream "I am fabulous!" or "I am excellent!" and expressions like that. It makes us feel excited and joyful. She tells girls that you should believe in what your heart tells you. Ms. Mahoney makes girls feel like they are very special to the world and not just one little piece of it. She teaches a class called "Girl Power." In the class, she does exercises and we copy her. These are important because they make our bodies strong. She also teaches about nutrition and eating healthy foods. She reminds us that it's important to keep ourselves healthy and strong. Sometimes she lets us use face paint and act like warriors. We think that's really fun. Sometimes Ms. Mahoney will help us try to find ways to be a better friend through better communication and understanding each other. Her students, like me, enjoy the class because it makes us feel really special in the world. She encourages us to believe in ourselves. I love her class! It makes me feel very special. That's why Ms. Mahoney is my Hopkinton Hero.

The PTA presents this award in a very meaningful way. The essay goes in a frame that also has quote, "A hundred years from now it will now matter, what my bank account was like, the state of health I was in, or the car that I drove. But the world may be different because I was important in the life of a child."

I was honored just to be nominated, much less actually become a Hopkinton Hero!

ABOUT THE AUTHOR

ERIN C. MAHONEY has over 29 years of experience in the health and fitness industry. After serving in the United States Air Force as a medic, Erin found a way to combine her healthcare background with her passion for fitness. She has been a certified personal trainer and certified group fitness instructor since 2001. She has held specialized certifications in yoga and kickboxing. Erin studied meditation, relaxation and stress reduction at the Center of Mindfulness at the University of Massachusetts Medical Center. Most recently Erin has moved into EFT (Emotional Freedom Technique) work in the form of Tapping.

Erin is the founder and creator of Girl Power Go which is an empowerment program for girls. This program was specifically designed to get girls ages 8 to 13 excited about being strong, self-confident, independent, and healthy. Erin saw a need for this important and relevant program and created unique four, six, and eight-week programs that give girls the tools they need to make good decisions in our ever demanding society. Erin combines life skills, fitness, positive thinking, creativity and fun into her program which reinforces her message to each girl that they can *Be Strong, Be Smart, Be Amazing!* Girl Power has been running successfully in many communities in her home state of Massachusetts. Erin has written this book in an effort to bring this program to the world! The demand for this program continues to grow and plans are in place to expand so that Erin and her Girl Power Go team might empower thousands of girls across the globe!

Erin incorporated her health and wellness company under the name of B3 Training, Inc. (Now called Girl Power Go), and with this, Erin has been able to expand and offer many programs. Girl Power Go offers a full range of services in the fitness field. Everything from group and one-on-one personal training, novice and marathon training running programs, and kids empowerment programs. Energy work and adult empowerment programs have been added as well as business and personal motivational coaching.

Girl Power Go has also joined forces with the Girl Scouts of Central and Western Massachusetts as a Community Partner. They love the message that the Girl Power Go program teaches, and Erin has created customized programs that give Daisies, Brownies, Juniors and Cadets the tools and experiences they need to develop leadership qualities through the key skills integral to Girl Scouting. Erin hopes to work with Girl Scouts all over the nation in the future.

Kid Power is an enrichment program created for boys and girls teaching them leadership, respect, and strength. This program works with kids during their school day to inspire them and help them build the foundation to make good decisions well beyond the classroom.

Erin is a seasoned running coach who has trained both novice and marathon runners. Having completed seven marathons herself, she is passionate about the sport. Serving on the Board of Directors for the Hopkinton Running Club as the Director of Training, Erin was instrumental in creating one of its most successful programs. In its first year, her "Couch to 5k" program successfully took over 60 non-runners and transformed them into runners. Now in its fourth year, Erin has grown this program to neighboring towns and has helped hundreds of runners reach their goals. Erin inspires her runners to *Be Courageous, Be Consistent, Be Committed.*

Erin lives in Milford, Massachusetts with her husband and two sons. She is passionate about what she does and takes pride in creating all of these programs that inspire and motivate people to uncover the power that they have within themselves. Her philosophy is that people have the ability to achieve any and all things that they set their minds to. It's her goal to help them get there!

APPENDIX: AFFIRMATIONS FOR CARDS

It's important to make these fun and beautiful, to capture the girls' interest and create value, and to have fun with it!

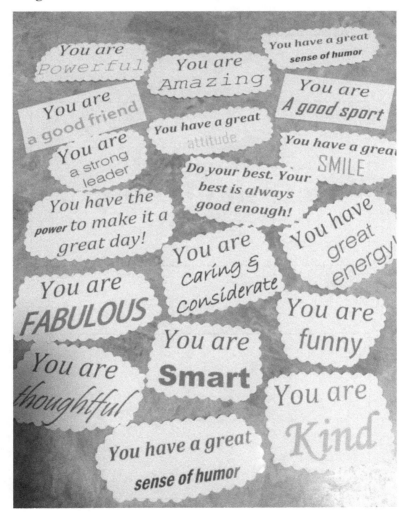

You are *smart!*

You are a
strong leader

You are **amazing**

You are *beautiful*

YOU ARE A
GOOD FRIEND

You are creative

You have a
great smile

You have a great
sense of humor

Do your best.
Your best is
always good enough!

You are funny

YOU HAVE THE
POWER TO MAKE
IT A GREAT DAY

You are kind

YOU ARE POWERFUL

You are *fabulous*

You are a
good sport

You have *great energy*

You have
Girl Power!

APPENDIX: BRACELETS AND BEADS

In the beginning of Girl Power I created and did an AMAZING project with them. We created Girl Power bracelets and I talked them through what this bracelet meant and would represent to/for them. I have attached the document I would give them with this activity. Pretty powerful stuff!

I discontinued this piece of the program because it was too expensive to maintain but it's certainly something that they could do within the workbook on their own or be added back into Girl Power classes in the future. It's so meaningful!

WHAT THE BEADS MEAN AND DEFINING WHO YOU WANT TO BE

1. The "You" bead is your birthstone and the first bead we select.

2. Then you choose the "primary stones" which represent the people you surround yourself with: your parents, siblings, close friends—the people that love and support you.

3. Next we take a look at the "personality and quality" beads. These are the beads that make you <u>YOU</u> or who you WANT to become.

   - Confident – Silver
   - Faith – Pearl
   - Girl Power – Rainbow Pink
   - Friendship and Friend – Dark Purple/Blue Rainbow
   - Honest and Trustworthy – Charcoal Gray
   - Helpful and Wise – Light Purple/Pink Rainbow
   - Nature Lover – Green

4. Charm Selection – Your bracelet will be closed off with a high quality sterling silver clasp and a charm of your choice. You will choose from the following charms:

   - Faith
   - Hope
   - Love
   - Peace
   - Joy

GET MORE GIRL POWER!

Bring Girl Power programs to your community or area!

Get cool Girl Power gear!

See ongoing live and online Girl Power programs
for young girls and women!

Become a Girl Power Go Certified Instructor!

Attend a Girl Power Conference or Retreat:
Meet Erin, and learn empowerment strategies
directly from her and her team!

Go to www.GirlPowerGo.com/Extras and get updated
information and news, see videos of actual Girl Power
classes, and get even more positive Girl Power vibes!

CPSIA information can be obtained
at www.ICGtesting.com
Printed in the USA
FFHW010939041118
49180143-53382FF